Why Malaysian Consumers *Prefer* Online Purchases

Jun Yew Goh

Copyright © 2024 by Jun Yew Goh

All rights reserved. No part of this monograph may be reproduced in any form, whether by electronic, mechanical or manual means, including information storage and retrieval systems, without permission in writing from the publisher, except by a reviewer who may quote brief passages in a review.

Cover design and layout

Bee Kiong Goh
beekiong@gmail.com

This monograph has been designed using images from Flaticon.com

PREFACE

Online purchase intention is a shopper's willingness to purchase things online. This piece of research on online purchase intention was done because of the gap in relevant literature available on factors affecting online purchase intentions related to e-commerce usage among consumers in Malaysia.

The factors studied as affecting online purchase intention among consumers in Malaysia were push factors (which are made up of purchasing power, time saving, perceived risk and frequency of online purchases) and pull factors (trust, price comparison, advertising and brand name). Age was also studied as a moderating variable on the relationship between push factors and pull factors in Malaysia. Physical hardcopies of the survey were distributed to generate responses from Malaysian consumers. Four hundred and twenty-four responses were collected and the data was analysed with SPSS Analysis. It was concluded that both push and pull factors have a strong positive impact on the online purchase intention of consumers in Malaysia while age can be proven positively and strongly to act as a moderating variable on the relationship between push factors and pull factors in Malaysia. For future research, extra information such as state residence of respondents needs to be collected.

This monograph is based on an undergraduate thesis project undertaken at the University of Wollongong Malaysia KDU (UOW Malaysia KDU) in May 2020 and I duly acknowledge the guidance extended by my supervisor, Associate Professor Dr Brian Wong See Mun.

Jun Yew GOH
Setia Alam, Selangor, Malaysia
15 April 2024

TABLE OF CONTENTS

Preface	I
Table of Contents	III
List of Tables	VI
List of Figures	VII
List of Abbreviations	VII

Chapter 1: Introduction

1.1	Introduction	2
1.2	Problem Statement	4
1.3	Research Questions	7
1.4	Research Objectives	8
1.5	Significance of Study	9
1.6	Project Flow and Timeline	11
1.7	Summary	12

Chapter 2: Literature Review

2.0	Literature Review	14
2.1	Consumer involvement in the Malaysian E-commerce Landscape	15
2.2	Motivational Theories	18
2.3	Motivation Factors in Online Purchase Behaviour	21
2.4	Online Purchase Intention	23
2.5	The Relationship between Push Factors and Online Purchase Intention	25

2.6	The Relationship between Pull Factors and Online Purchase Intention	32
2.7	Age and its moderating impact on the relationship between push and pull factors with Online Purchase Intention	38
2.8	Conceptual Framework	41
2.9	Summary	43

Chapter 3: Methodology

3.0	Methodology	46
3.1	Research Method	47
3.2	Research Design	50
3.3	Questionnaire Development	52
3.4	Sampling Method	53
3.5	Data Collection	56
3.6	Data Analysis	58
3.6.1	Pilot Test	61
3.7	Summary	63

Chapter 4: Results

4.0	Results	66
4.1.1	Demographics of the respondents	67
4.1.2	Descriptive Analysis	72
4.2.1	Normality Tests for Push Factors, Pull Factors and Online Purchase Intention	80

4.2.2 Cronbach's Alpha tests	85
4.2.3 Multiple Regression Analysis	87
4.3 Summary	101

Chapter 5: Conclusion

5.0 Conclusion	106
5.1 Summary of analysis done on Research Objectives	107
5.1.1 Push Factors and Pull Factors for the project	107
5.1.2 Push factors and Online Purchase Intention	109
5.1.3 Pull factors and Online Purchase Intention	112
5.1.4 The impact of age as the moderating variable on the relationship between Push Factors / Pull Factors and Online Purchase Intention	114
5.2 Significance of the Study	117
5.3 Limitations	118
5.4 Recommendations	119
5.5 Conclusion	120
References	123
Appendix A	153
Appendix B	167
Appendix C	201
Appendix D	213
Appendix E	233

LIST OF TABLES

Table 2.1	22
Table 3.1	55
Table 3.2	61
Table 4.1.1	67
Table 4.1.2	67
Table 4.1.3	68
Table 4.1.4	69
Table 4.1.5	70
Table 4.1.6	70
Table 4.1.7	73
Table 4.1.8	74
Table 4.1.9	75
Table 4.1.10	76
Table 4.1.11	77
Table 4.1.12	77
Table 4.2.1	81
Table 4.2.2	83
Table 4.2.3	84
Table 4.2.4	86
Table 4.2.5	88
Table 4.2.6	89
Table 4.2.7	90

Table 4.2.8	92
Table 4.2.9	93
Table 4.2.10	94
Table 4.2.11	96
Table 4.2.12	98

LIST OF FIGURES

Figure 1.1	11
Figure E1	234
Figure E2	234
Figure E3	235
Figure E4	236
Figure E5	237
Figure E6	238

LIST OF ABBREVIATIONS

RM = Ringgit Malaysia (Bavanandan et al, 2016)

CHAPTER 1

INTRODUCTION

1.1 Introduction

By definition, online purchase intention can be stated as a shopper's willingness to purchase a product online and why or how much is the shopper willing to buy the aforementioned product online (Phang, Lee and Nabilah, 2019).

Online purchase intention of shoppers can be linked to e-commerce (Escobar-Rodríguez and Bonsón-Fernández, 2017), and since there is an increase in the importance of e-commerce nowadays, assisted by the increased global availability of the Internet (Arshad, Ibrahim and Chook, 2016) to conduct e-commerce transactions that they are developing and influencing global industries quickly (Ocloo et al, 2018), a study of the online purchase intention of consumers is more necessary nowadays (Phang, Lee and Nabilah, 2019). Nevertheless, the usage of e-commerce is more successful in generating benefits for developed countries than developing countries (Lim, Baharudin and Low, 2016).

E-commerce usage by Malaysian businesses, on average, has increased the revenue of the Malaysian economy from e-commerce, with an increase in e-commerce generated revenue by RM 49.6 billion between 2015 and 2017 (The Star, 2019). In the future, e-commerce may be necessary for businesses to maintain competitiveness without losing out (Ocloo et al, 2018) and to compete against bigger businesses (Kartiwi et al, 2018), which makes the study of online purchase intentions among consumers in Malaysia more important (Escobar-Rodríguez and Bonsón-Fernández, 2017).

Therefore, this research aims to understand the drivers of online purchase intention among consumers in Malaysia.

1.2 Problem Statement

———

This research on online purchase intentions is done because there is a problem, a gap in relevant literature available on factors affecting online purchase intentions related to e-commerce usage among consumers in Malaysia. This is due to the lack of recent research done on these factors affecting online purchase intentions in the Malaysian context, especially with regard to time saving (Fatin, Noor and Kalsitinoor, 2019) and price comparison (Mohd Fawzy et al, 2018).

This means that people can find it difficult to see the reasons behind the present levels of online purchase intention for e-commerce usage in Malaysia and device solutions to increase levels of online purchase intention for e-commerce usage in Malaysia based on time saving and price comparison (Mohd Fawzy et al, 2018). Therefore, research is being done in order to cover the gap in recent and relevant literature available on factors which affect online purchase intentions among consumers in Malaysia (Mohd Fawzy et al, 2018).

In addition, push and pull factors need to be studied in this research because they look at the exact factors and types of motivations behind people's decision making (Mkubukeli and Cronje, 2018). There is a gap in relevant literature available which studies both push and pull factors in the context of impacting online purchase intentions associated with e-commerce usage among consumers in Malaysia. This is because there is a lack of research done on how and which push and pull factors influence the motivation of people in their intention to purchase things online, especially in the Malaysian context (Abdul Kadir et al, 2019). As a result, people can find it difficult to evaluate the motivation of people having online purchase intentions for e-commerce usage in Malaysia and the influence of motivation on the factors (push factors and pull factors) behind these people's online purchase intentions (Said and Maryono, 2018) in both internal and external motivation (Mkubukeli and Cronje, 2018). Therefore, research is being done to cover the gap caused by the lack of relevant and recent literature available on how and which push and pull factors affect online purchase intentions in Malaysia with external and internal motivation respectively (Mkubukeli and Cronje, 2018).

Also, age will be studied as a moderating variable in this monograph (Liebana-Cabanillas and Alonso-Dos-Santos, 2017). Age as a moderating variable needs to be studied here to fill the gap in literature available on the role of age as a moderating variable on the relationship between factors affecting online purchase intentions and online purchase intentions within the Malaysian context. This can cause difficulty in observing the moderating impact of age on the relationship between factors influencing consumers' online purchase intentions and these consumers' online purchase intentions in the current Malaysian context (Liebana-Cabanillas and Alonso-Dos-Santos, 2017). Therefore, research is being done to cover the gap due to the lack of relevant and recent literature available on the role of age as a moderating variable affecting the relationship between factors affecting online purchase intentions and online purchase intentions among consumers in Malaysia (Liebana-Cabanillas and Alonso-Dos-Santos, 2017).

1.3 Research Questions

Research questions to be asked based on the problem statement above are:

RQ1: What are the push and pull factors driving online purchase intentions among consumers in Malaysia?

RQ2: What is the relationship between push factors and the driving of online purchase intentions among consumers in Malaysia?

RQ3: What is the relationship between pull factors and the driving of online purchase intentions among consumers in Malaysia?

RQ4: What is the moderating effect of age on the relationship between the motivation factors and the driving of online purchase intentions among consumers in Malaysia?

1.4 Research Objectives

Based on the research questions, the study is governed by the following research objectives:

RO1) To determine the push and pull factors driving the online purchase intentions among consumers in Malaysia.

RO2) To determine the relationship between push factors and the driving of online purchase intentions among consumers in Malaysia.

RO3) To determine the relationship between pull factors and the driving of online purchase intentions among consumers in Malaysia.

RO4) To determine the moderating effect of age on the relationship between the motivation factors and the driving of online purchase intentions among consumers in Malaysia.

1.5 Significance of Study

The significance of study for this monograph is to study the factors affecting online purchase intention among consumers in Malaysia. This is to generate solutions from businesses for improving e-commerce usage among consumers in Malaysia. The solutions are to be collected by asking questions about the reasons affecting the online purchase intentions of online shoppers in Malaysia. It is expected that the research will assist businesses in modifying their operations and surveyed consumers in Malaysia in changing their habits to change the online purchase intentions of online shoppers in Malaysia in order to increase e-commerce usage in Malaysia (in percentage of Malaysia's population and number of e-commerce users in Malaysia).

Another reason for the study's significance is to evaluate how age moderates the impact of independent variables for the research's dependent variable (online purchase intention). This is to help online businesses target consumers more effectively and accurately based on their age after looking at the factors affecting e-commerce usage among consumers in Malaysia as they modify their operations to ensure more online consumers in Malaysia use e-commerce by changing their online purchase intentions. The age of respondents will be obtained by asking the same online shoppers previously interviewed for the research on how their age affected the relationship between their purchasing power, time saving, price comparison and frequency of online purchases and their online purchase intention.

Chapter 1: Introduction

1.6 Project Flow and Timeline

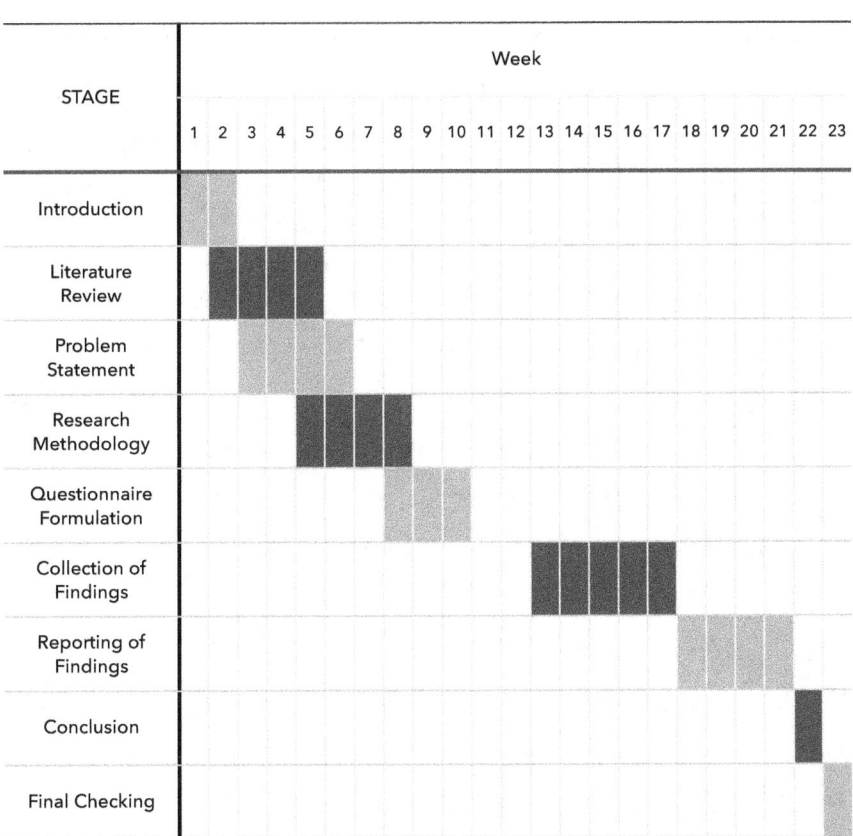

Figure 1.1: Figure for Project Flow and timeline

The figure above is the intended project flow and timeline for this research.

1.7 Summary

———

In conclusion, online purchase intention is a shopper's willingness to purchase a product online and why or how much is the shopper willing to buy the aforementioned product online (Phang, Lee and Nabilah, 2019).

This research is undertaken to look at the factors which can determine the online purchase intentions of consumers in Malaysia and cover gaps in recent literature related to how these factors influence the online purchase intentions of consumers in Malaysia. This is to assist in producing solutions for increasing levels of online purchase intention for e-commerce usage in Malaysia (Mohd Fawzy et al, 2018).

These factors are push and pull factors (Mkubukeli and Cronje, 2018), with age acting as a moderating variable in the relationship between the same push and pull factors and online purchase intentions (Liebana-Cabanillas and Alonso-Dos-Santos, 2017).

CHAPTER 2

LITERATURE REVIEW

2.0 Literature Review

E-commerce is defined as the online purchase and selling of products (Sanwal, Avasthi and Saxena, 2016). E-commerce can also be defined as business activities done through electronic mediums such as product promotions or technology usage such as e-mail and web portal, according to Lim, Baharudin and Low (2016), while Arshad et al (2018) defined e-commerce as how business information is distributed on the Internet to maintain business relationships and to do business transactions.

Given that this research is about the development of e-commerce in Malaysia, this development needs to be looked at from the potential of the Malaysian market for e-commerce development and the benefits of using e-commerce (Saif-Ur-Rehman and Rizwan, 2016), which will be determined by surveys and questionnaires (Creswell, 2014) to see why and how much e-commerce is used in Malaysia and how its usage in Malaysia can be improved (Saif-Ur-Rehman and Rizwan, 2016).

Chapter 2: Literature Review

2.1 Consumer involvement in the Malaysian E-commerce Landscape

---

E-commerce has benefitted big companies in improving business efficiency (Saif-Ur-Rehman and Rizwan, 2016). Smaller companies can also benefit from e-commerce in factors such as support for transactions (Lim, Baharudin and Low, 2016) and customer demand (Xu and Quaddus (2009), as stated by Saif-Ur-Rehman and Rizwan (2016)). In the future, e-commerce may be needed by a business to avoid losing competitiveness without e-commerce usage (Ocloo et al, 2018). Therefore, research can be done to prove that e-commerce benefits Malaysia's businesses and to study e-commerce usage and why e-commerce usage occurs in Malaysia based on the recorded benefits of e-commerce usage (Kartiwi et al, 2018).

In Malaysia, the usage of e-commerce has been favourable in potential, with a Nielsen Global Online Survey 2014 finding that more than 60% of Malaysian shoppers had used e-commerce (Jamil and Mimi, 2016). E-commerce is most favoured by surveyed Malaysians for the reason of saving time (Mohd Fawzy et al, 2018). It must be noted that for SME's, e-commerce is a quite recent thing, making e-commerce providers and information technology experts to assist the SME's on e-commerce usage necessary (Arshad et al, 2018). With the sample size not restricted by university studies, potential for e-commerce usage among consumers in Malaysia can be better judged with the factors for e-commerce preference from the study by Mohd Fawzy et al (2018) than from the study of Lim et al (2015). Research done has proven that a higher purchasing power increases the potential for e-commerce usage among consumers in Malaysia (Lim, Azizah and Ramayah, 2015). In addition, a study about perceived risk among consumers in Malaysia found that perceived risk related to e-commerce usage can impact e-commerce usage among consumers in Malaysia (Noorshella et al, 2019). A study by Tan (2018) found that the frequency of online purchases of consumers in Malaysia also affects the e-commerce usage of these consumers.

Trust has been found to affect e-commerce usage among consumers in Malaysia (Fatin, Noor and Kalsitinoor, 2019). Mohd Fawzy et al (2018) found that the facilitation of price comparison is a major reason why e-commerce is favoured by Malaysians. Also, advertising (Kowang et al, 2019) and brand name are factors positively affecting e-commerce usage among consumers in Malaysia (Azrin, Tarofder and Azam, 2018).

Despite the potential for e-commerce adoption in Malaysia, there are barriers to the adoption of e-commerce in Malaysia, which are organizational barriers, technical barriers, regulatory and legal barriers, financial barriers and behavioural barriers (Saif-Ur-Rehman and Rizwan, 2016), in addition to defective products, lack of warranties, poor security, cheating by sellers and poor Internet connection (Mohd Fawzy et al, 2018). Also, research done did suggest that it is difficult for managers to reap the benefits of e-commerce (Akter and Wamba, 2016). This has supported a hypothesis that e-commerce does not benefit organizational performance (Oladapo and Onyeaso, 2018), and therefore contradicts the belief that e-commerce is beneficial for workplace performance (Sanwal, Avasthi and Saxena, 2016). This is especially in the event a website's success in using e-commerce cannot be measured properly, resulting in ineffective e-commerce activities with few benefits generated (Ghandour, 2015).

2.2 Motivational Theories

There are several motivational theories which will be canvassed for this monograph. The motivation to be found in these motivational theories provides reasons for people to do things (Uysal, Aydemir and Genc, 2017). An example of a motivational theory to be used is Maslow's Hierarchy of Needs (Ahmed, 2017). Maslow's Hierarchy of Needs, as developed by Abraham Maslow (Uysal, Aydemir and Genc, 2017), is a motivational theory which assumes that people's motivations are determined by their exact needs and therefore, these needs can affect how they are motivated to act (Ahmed, 2017). In Maslow's Hierarchy of Needs, as people's needs in one level of Maslow's Hierarchy of Needs are satisfied, the people tend to look for needs in the next highest level of the hierarchy as that hierarchy level dominates people's motivation until all their needs in the hierarchy level are satisfied and only then will these people look to the next level of needs (Uysal, Aydemir and Genc, 2017). In Maslow's Hierarchy of Needs, there are five levels of needs, these levels being comprised of psychological needs, safety needs, social needs, esteem needs and self-actualization needs (Uysal, Aydemir and Genc, 2017).

Theory X, Theory Y and Theory Z are motivational theories which will also be looked at as they look at how people are motivated (Aithal and Kumar, 2016). Douglas McGregor developed Theory X and Theory Y to look at workforce motivation (Hattangadi, 2015).

Theory X assumes that people tend to be lazy, passive and lacking in motivation without the assistance of others while Theory Y assumes that people are hardworking, active and motivated to change their environment by themselves (Aithal and Kumar, 2016). In addition, Theory Z, developed by William Ouchi, believed that motivation for workforce employees' actions is dependent on employee loyalty to their company, provided that these employees have their jobs in their company for life as long as there is an emphasis on these employees' well-being at and outside work (Aithal and Kumar, 2016).

Another theory of motivation to be used is the push and pull theory of motivation, which looks at the incentives generated by motivation to cause people to do things (Mkubukeli and Cronje, 2018). All the above theories look at how the behaviour of people is affected by motivation (Said and Maryono, 2018).

This research will use the push and pull theory of motivation to look at the exact motives behind the online purchase intentions of online shoppers in Malaysia, and this theory is made of push factors and pull factors (Mkubukeli and Cronje, 2018). The push factors of the push and pull theory force needed action among people from external factors and the pull factors of the push and pull theory create attraction by encouraging action among people through internal incentives generated by motivation (Mkubukeli and Cronje, 2018). However, a study by Thirumoorthi and Wong (2015) found that people's actions are pushed by internal forces acting as push factors and pulled by external forces acting as pull factors.

In addition, push factors come from the minds of people acting on push factors and based on the internal desires of people who act based on these desires to satisfy needs while pull factors are external factors to people which contribute to these people's desire to do things (Thirumoorthi and Wong, 2015). Although treated separately for the purposes of research, push and pull factors are found by other researchers to be connected (Thirumoorthi and Wong, 2015). They can be used to determine the reasons and the motives behind the online purchase intentions of online shoppers in Malaysia (Mkubukeli and Cronje, 2018). It must be noted that the push and pull theory of motivation is the most relevant theory to be selected for this research as it looks at how people are motivated by internal and external incentives to do things (Mkubukeli and Cronje, 2018). As this monograph examines at internal and external incentives encouraging people's online purchase intention, the push and pull theory is the most appropriate motivation theory for the project (Mkubukeli and Cronje, 2018), unlike Maslow's Hierarchy of Needs as it looks at how people are motivated by personal needs (Ahmed, 2017) and Theory X, Theory Y and Theory Z, which look at people's motivation to do things (Aithal and Kumar, 2016).

2.3 Motivation Factors in Online Purchase Behaviour

With regard to the push factors and related objective for this research, a push factor is purchasing power and how it drives online purchase intentions in Malaysia (Lim, Azizah and Ramayah, 2015) as a push factor (Mkubukeli and Cronje, 2018). Another push factor here (Mkubukeli and Cronje, 2018) is the impact of time saving on online purchase intentions among surveyed consumers in Malaysia (Mohd Fawzy et al, 2018). Perceived risk is another push factor to be investigated for its relation to online purchase intentions (Mazzini, Rohani and Salwana, 2016). The impact of frequency of online purchases on online purchase intentions by surveyed consumers in Malaysia is another push factor to be investigated for the purpose of this monograph (Lim et al, 2015).

This monograph also uses pull factors to generate objectives for research (Mkubukeli and Cronje, 2018). One of this monograph's pull factors is trust, which will be investigated for its impact on online purchase intentions of consumers in Malaysia involved in the research (Bulut, 2015). The impact of price comparison on online purchase intentions among surveyed consumers in Malaysia is another pull factor here (Mohd Fawzy et al, 2018). The effects of advertising as a pull factor on online purchase intentions in Malaysia will be investigated for this monograph (Ekpe, Adubasim and Adim, 2016).

Another pull factor here is the consequences of brand name on online purchase intentions in Malaysia (Ghouri, ul Haq and Khan, 2017).

This monograph also has the objective of investigating the moderating variable of determining the role of age on the relationship between push factors and pull factors with online purchase intentions among surveyed consumers in Malaysia (Tanadi, Samadi and Gharleghi, 2015).

Table 2.1: A table of push factors and pull factors used.

Push Factors Affecting Online Purchase Intentions Among Customers In Malaysia	Pull Factors Affecting Online Purchase Intentions Among Customers In Malaysia
Purchasing power (Lim, Azizah and Ramayah, 2015).	Trust (Bulut, 2015).
Time Saving (Mohd Fawzy et al, 2018).	Price comparison (Mohd Fawzy et al, 2018).
Perceived risk (Mazzini, Rohani and Salwana, 2016).	Advertising (Ekpe, Adubasim and Adim, 2016).
Frequency of online purchases (Lim et al, 2015).	Brand Name (Ghouri, ul Haq and Khan, 2017).

2.4 Online Purchase Intention

The online purchase intention of shoppers can be linked to e-commerce (Escobar-Rodríguez and Bonsón-Fernández, 2017). By definition, online purchase intention is a shopper's willingness to purchase a product online and why or how much is the shopper willing to buy the aforementioned product online (Phang, Lee and Nabilah, 2019). The growth of e-commerce has made an analysis of online purchase intention more necessary due to the increase in online purchases generated by e-commerce (Phang, Lee and Nabilah, 2019). Fishbein and Ajzen (1975), as stated by Kaur, Wadera and Sethi (2018), mentioned that intentions predict behaviour since intentions are caused by a person's subjective norm of behaviour and attitude and therefore, online purchase intentions can affect consumer buying behaviour, with those having online purchase intentions to buy a product more willing to buy a product than those without online purchase intentions to buy the same product (Kaur, Wadera and Sethi, 2018). As online purchase intentions can determine a person's willingness to buy things online with some predictive usefulness, studying the factors affecting online purchase intentions is essential (Kaur, Wadera and Sethi, 2018).

Online purchase intention can also be stated as a person's attitude towards an online purchase and its associated subjective norms (Nor Hazlin, Nurazariah and Hafizzah, 2016). It can be used to predict behaviour of customers in future purchase decisions and configure their attitudes (Nor Hazlin, Nurazariah and Hafizzah, 2016). For products and services, purchase intentions are useful in predicting their sales (Nor Hazlin, Nurazariah and Hafizzah, 2016). It must be noted that a study of online purchase intentions is important in today's marketing as companies use online purchase intentions to predict sold products' sales potential (Phang, Lee and Nabilah, 2019). According to Shanthi and Kannaiah (2015), online purchase intentions are determined by utilitarianism, ease of use, enjoyment, situational factors, trust in online shopping and earlier experiences with online shopping. In addition, online purchase intentions among online shoppers in Malaysia can be defined by purchasing power, time saving, price comparison (Mohd Fawzy et al, 2018) and the frequency of previous online shopping experiences (Lim et al, 2015).

2.5 The Relationship between Push Factors and Online Purchase Intention

---

This section is about push factors and how they influence online purchase intention (Mkubukeli and Cronje, 2018). The relationship between the purchasing power of online shoppers and online purchase intention will be first looked at in this section (Majid and Firend, 2017). Suryanegara, Andriyanto and Winarko (2017) stated that purchasing power refers to the total money that can be spent daily or monthly. According to Majid and Firend (2017), it was found that the purchasing power of the respondents to their survey had no effect on their online purchase intention. In addition, various factors can reduce the effect of purchasing power on online purchase intentions (Meera and Gayathri, 2018). However, a study by Liu and Wu (2019) found that purchasing power will affect the online purchase intentions of the survey's respondents.

A higher purchasing power, which can affect online purchase intentions (Chang and Chao, 2018), can be determined by a higher income (Irianto, 2015). Abu-Shamaa, Abu-Shanab and Khasawneh (2016) stated that a higher income can be linked to an increased intention to purchase things online. In addition, a higher income among people will increase their willingness to buy things from the Internet (Li and Hou, 2019). It must be noted that in Malaysia, higher purchasing power among consumers can determine online purchase intentions (Lim, Azizah and Ramayah, 2015).

A higher purchasing power can be linked to more goods consumed with online shopping and a higher inclination towards a positive online purchase intention (Agyapong, 2018). Tseng et al (2017) stated that consumers' purchasing power can produce a significant positive impact on the online purchase intention of these consumers at e-commerce shops, especially if they can bargain and get better prices for these shops' products with the shops' marketing efforts' assistance. After all, an increased purchasing power among young people can be linked to increased e-commerce activities (Duffett, 2017), which can be linked in turn to a higher online purchase intention (Escobar-Rodríguez and Bonsón-Fernández, 2017).

Next, the relationship between the ability of online shopping to save online shoppers' time and online purchase intention will also be evaluated (Majid and Firend, 2017). Purchasing online generally saves time compared to other methods of purchases (Jadhav and Khanna, 2016), therefore, time saving is important in determining online purchase intentions (Kharel, 2018). It must be noted that time saving is a reason why younger people do online shopping more frequently than older people (Li and Hou, 2019).

In fact, time saving has been found in a survey by Kharel (2018) to be the most crucial factor affecting online purchase intention of survey respondents. This is because online purchases save people the time needed to go shopping away from home by allowing online purchases of shoppers to be done from home, positively influencing online purchase intentions (Rrumbullaku and Kume, 2017). A study by Suhan (2015) also found that the assumption that online shopping saves time of those who do online shopping for other activities by allowing shopping to be done from home is believed by 79.2% of the study's respondents. In addition, Sharma (2017) stated that online shopping is advantageous in time saving by allowing purchases to be made just by clicking on a mouse and getting a certain list of products to be purchased in mind, in addition to contributing to effort conservation. Therefore, it is not surprising that a study by Mohd Fawzy et al (2018) found that time saving was the most important reason for Malaysians involved in the study to have higher online purchase intentions.

That said, despite the time savings generated by online shopping compared to other shopping methods, the ability to conduct online shopping depends on the availability of Internet connections, which will be problematic in rural areas (Shanthi and Kannaiah, 2015). Also, an online study by Vyas and Bissa (2017) found that only 10% of its respondents chose online shopping for time saving, with the same study finding out that online shopping does not guarantee time saving compared to other modes of shopping with people who do online shopping looking for products which these people have no motivation for buying after purchasing with online shopping, suggesting that time saving is not a major online purchase intention for these people when they conduct online shopping. Finally, the study of Suhan (2015) found that while online shopping saves time, there is an excessive amount of time spent on delivering products purchased by online shopping to the product's purchasers, as it found that 57.5% of the study's respondents believed that too much time has been spent delivering products purchased by online shopping. These findings suggest that time saving as a reason for encouraging online purchase intentions is not guaranteed (Suhan, 2015).

The relationship between perceived risk and online purchase intention will also be studied (Mazzini, Rohani and Salwana, 2016). By definition, perceived risk is the subjective expectation of consumers in experiencing losses to achieve what the consumer wants (Liew and Falahat, 2019). There is evidence that perceived risk can affect shoppers' online purchase intentions, albeit not in a negative manner based on a study's results (Mazzini, Rohani and Salwana, 2016). Increased perceived risk has been associated with a negative attitude towards online purchase intention and likelihood to purchase things on the Internet because of fears of uncertainty with the likelihood of serious outcomes and negative intentions occurring during online purchases (Mazzini, Rohani and Salwana, 2016).

Reasons for why perceived risk is an issue affecting online purchases and online purchase intention include lack of personal contact with online purchases, security of payment and the need to change purchasing habits for online purchases, which involve change and risk (Mazzini, Rohani and Salwana, 2016). Tanadi, Samadi and Gharleghi (2015) found that perceived risk can be found in online shopping at a higher likelihood than traditional shopping and despite the progress in online shopping, can result in hesitation in using online shopping and online purchase intentions. Also, a study in Malaysia found that perceived risk can negatively influence online purchase intentions when perceived risk can be associated with products to be purchased from online stores due to the likelihood of purchasing the wrong products (Ariffin, Mohan and Goh, 2018).

Zhao, Deng and Zhou (2017) found that perceived risk does mediate the online purchase intentions for products, although to a lesser extent than perceived value. Ariffin, Mohan and Goh (2018) also found that perceived risk does negatively impact the online purchase intentions for products in a negative manner, with perceived risk in the forms of financial risk, security risk and time risk being the forms of perceived risk negatively affecting the online purchase intentions. Kim and Koo (2016), however, found that perceived risk has an insignificant consequence on online purchase intentions. Also, Chen, Yan and Fan (2015) found that perceived risk faced by customers online does affect purchase intentions of these customers, although to a slight extent.

Online purchase intentions of shoppers can also be determined by their frequency of previous online purchases (Selvaraju and

Karthikeyan, 2016). This is because a study by Wu and Tsai (2017) suggested that those more experienced in online purchasing will have a higher intention of shopping online, especially if they use the Internet frequently and skilfully. Kanchan, Kumar and Gupta (2015) found that the higher the frequency of purchasing things online by people, the higher the online purchase intentions for these people, noting that the frequency of purchasing things online by people is based on technology familiarity. It must be noted that a study by Selvaraju and Karthikeyan (2016) found that frequency of online purchases contributed to online purchase intentions of surveyed customers through these customers finding increased ease of use for online shopping with frequency of online purchases, with the study finding that ease of use has a bigger effect than usefulness, product features and perceived risk. In addition, a study by Arulkumar and Kannaiah (2015) found that among its surveyed respondents, a higher frequency of online purchases done by these respondents determined higher online purchase intentions based on shopping experience level.

However, a study by Sethna, Hazari and Bergiel (2017) found that more frequent online purchases cannot be associated with higher online purchase intentions for females and males responding to the study. A study by Maia et al (2018) also found that higher online purchase intentions cannot be significantly determined by frequent online purchases. In Malaysia, a study by Lim et al (2015) also found that there is no significant impact from more frequent online purchases on online purchase intentions.

From the literature review above, the following hypothesis is proposed:

H1: There is a positive relationship between push factors and online purchase intention.

2.6 The Relationship between Pull Factors and Online Purchase Intention

---

This section studies pull factors and their effect on online purchase intention (Mkubukeli and Cronje, 2018). The relationship between trust and online purchase intentions will be evaluated first (Bulut, 2015). By definition, trust in online purchase intention is the online customer's initiative in taking action although the action leaves the customer vulnerable to and relying on his seller (Bulut, 2015). Trust is a factor which determines online purchase intentions given the developments in online shopping and e-commerce over the last ten years that it is important as it determines customer retention in online shopping (Rezaei, Emami and Valaei, 2016). Customers involved in online shopping tend to have lower trust with the activity as online shopping, compared to conventional shopping, has security and privacy problems and brings in a more complicated assessment of the product to be purchased, and this influences their online purchase intention (Bulut, 2015). The three major determinants of trust which determine higher online purchase intentions with increased trust are competence, integrity and benevolence (Oliveria et al, 2017). A study by Escobar-Rodríguez and Bonsón-Fernández (2017) found that trust is important (when mediated by perceived security and time saving) in determining online purchase intentions of the study's respondents. Hong (2015) also found that trust has a positive influence on a consumer's online purchase intention.

In addition, Bulut (2015) found that website trust produces a major impact on the online purchase intention of online customers compared to loyalty. This can be assisted by the fact that trust in a website can reduce uncertainties among consumers with regard to online shopping, which can improve consumers' online purchase intention towards online shopping with reduced uncertainties (Bulut, 2015). Customer trust in online shopping and subsequent online purchase intention can be determined by online shopping vendor trustworthiness and the attractiveness of the vendor's website (Adiwijaya, 2015), besides confidence in online sellers (Abdul Kadir et al, 2019). In Malaysia, customer trust in online shopping based on business trustworthiness has been needed to generate online purchase intentions, showing that trust is a major factor in determining online purchase intentions (Fatin, Noor and Kalsitinoor, 2019).

It must be noted that trust in online purchase intentions can be negatively impacted by perceived risk (Silva et al, 2019). Another factor affecting trust in online shopping is the risk of hacking, which can lower security in online shopping that online purchase intentions are reduced (Chakraborty et al, 2016). Finally, trust in online shopping environments can determine and increase online purchase intentions by increasing information seeking, familiarity and perceptions of social presence with these online shopping environments (Hajli et al, 2017).

Price comparison can also determine the online purchase intentions of shoppers (Mohd Fawzy et al, 2018). By definition, price comparison refers to the comparison of prices between two or more products with the prices (Vogler, Schneider and Zimmermann, 2017). It must be noted that a study by Nurlaily, Noermijati and Hussein (2017) did find the importance of price comparison on the online purchase intentions of shoppers, as the results generated from the study's survey showed that price comparison was among the main reasons for repurchase intentions among online shoppers with online social media. Price comparison is a reason affecting online purchase intentions because people, especially younger people, generally choose to do online purchases to save money compared to other methods of product purchases (Li and Hou, 2019).

In addition, Mohd Fawzy et al (2018) found in their survey that price comparison was a major factor in determining online purchase intentions of the survey's Malaysian respondents. Beranek, Remes and Nydl (2017) did find that online purchase intentions of shoppers were positively influenced by price comparison websites as these websites would provide price overviews for products to allow products to be purchased by these shoppers to be compared with regard to price, in addition to assisting shoppers in searching for products and determining purchase intentions based on perception of quality of delivery, price consciousness, perception of risk and reputation according to these online buyers. Finally, in China, it was found that the ability to compare prices with online shopping has contributed to higher online purchase intentions among its customers, especially for cheaper products (Khan, Liang and Shahzad, 2015).

Advertising is another factor which can determine people's online purchase intentions, given that Weng (2015) found that Internet advertising can improve online purchase intentions by improving perceived value and perceived risks associated with online shops. A study by Ekpe, Adubasim and Adim (2016) noticed a positive relationship between advertising and online purchase intentions. The study noted that advertising will positively affect online purchase intentions for a product through increased product exposure to the advertised product and the exposure's impact on the thinking of customers who have seen the product advertised with influences on these customers' attitudes, awareness and purchase intentions (Ekpe, Adubasim and Adim, 2016).

It must be noted that advertising can increase online purchase intentions when it targets its target market with precise targeting to the target market compared to regular online advertising (Watts, 2016) and by creating a brand image for products to be purchased online (Kowang et al, 2019). In addition, advertising has been found to be a crucial factor in driving online purchase intentions in China by Zhao and Wan (2017). However, Shaouf, Lu and Li (2016) found that advertising has no direct effect on people's online purchase intentions. Also, a study on the online purchase intention of Malaysian consumers found that advertising has no impact on these consumers' online purchase intention (Kowang et al, 2019).

The final pull factor to be evaluated to study the relationship between pull factors and online purchase intentions is brand name (Faryabi, Fesaghandis and Saed, 2015). By definition, brand name refers to a name which leads to association with a brand through a positive brand image (Faryabi, Fesaghandis and Saed, 2015). A study done by Ghouri, ul Haq and Khan (2017) found that the brand name associated with products has significant impacts on people's online purchase intentions. This is because when conducting online purchases, people generally buy products online with the assistance of brand names instead of product information (Ghouri, ul Haq and Khan, 2017). It must be noted that the impact of brand names on online purchase intentions and brand consciousness is higher nowadays and recently compared to the past (Ghouri, ul Haq and Khan, 2017). Brand names, when assisted by producing a sense of visual or mental familiarity with the brand, can determine the favourable or unfavourable consumer attitudes to a brand (Mostafa and Elseidi, 2018), which can determine online purchase intentions for the same brand's products as a result (Faryabi, Fesaghandis and Saed, 2015). When there is higher perceived value or affordability in a product's brand name, that brand name can lead to higher online purchase intentions for the product (Faryabi, Fesaghandis and Saed, 2015).

Other reasons why brand names can affect online purchase intentions are the provision of information with brand names (if recognizable) through word-of-mouth communication, earlier purchases or product usage and advertising related to the brand names to customers having online purchase intentions for products owned by the brands with these brand names (Faryabi, Fesaghandis and Saed, 2015). This is because customers tend to process products' brand names with more recognizable brand names and pay attention to these brand names more frequently than for products with less recognizable brand names (Faryabi, Fesaghandis and Saed, 2015). In addition, in Malaysia, Azrin, Tarofder and Azam (2018) found that increased brand name familiarity among people has increased their online purchase intentions. This is through the factor of brand name association with high quality products (Azrin, Tarofder and Azam, 2018).

From the literature review above, the following hypothesis is proposed:

H2: There is a positive relationship between pull factors and online purchase intention.

2.7 Age and its moderating impact on the relationship between push and pull factors with Online Purchase Intention

―――

Age can be seen as a moderating variable affecting online purchase intentions, based on a study which found that age could affect the online purchase intentions of the study's respondents through moderating usefulness, social image and subjective norms (Liebana-Cabanillas and Alonso-Dos-Santos, 2017). This means that age moderates the influence of the aforementioned study's independent variables on its dependent variable of online purchase intentions (Creswell, 2014). For online activities such as online purchases, age is an important variable which determines familiarity with and adoption of these online activities (Schurink, 2019). Despite this, Kamboj and Rahman (2016) found that act does not have a significant impact on consumers' online purchase intentions. For this research, age will moderate the impact of the independent variables of purchasing power (Liu and Wu, 2019), time saving (Shanthi and Kannaiah, 2015), perceived risk (Khan, Liang and Shahzad, 2015) and frequency of online purchases (Kanchan, Kumar and Gupta, 2015) on the dependent variable of online purchase intentions (Kanchan, Kumar and Gupta, 2015). In addition, for this research, age will moderate the impact of the independent variables of trust (Bulut, 2015), price comparison (Nurlaily, Noermijati and Hussein, 2017), advertising (Ekpe, Adubasim and Adim, 2016) and brand name (Faryabi,

Fesaghandis and Saed, 2015) on the dependent variable of online purchase intentions (Kanchan, Kumar and Gupta, 2015).

A study involving Malaysian students by Sharifi Fard et al (2016) found that age acts as a moderating variable with significant effects only for the relationship between performance expectancy and online purchase intention. In addition, younger people in age have higher online purchase intentions than older people since they will be more likely to do online shopping than older people, assisted by an initiative among these younger people to save money than older people, besides spending more time and being more likely to find things online, trust e-commerce and be earlier (Li and Hou, 2019) and heavier users of e-commerce (Agudo-Peregrina, Acquila-Natale and Hernandez-Garcia, 2015).

As a moderating variable, age controls the relations between mental accounts and online purchase intentions (Li and Hou, 2019). Also, age is usable as a moderating variable in determining online purchase intentions because people can have socio-cognitive differences depending on their age (Agudo-Peregrina, Acquila-Natale and Hernandez-Garcia, 2015).

Age as a moderating variable does weaken the relationship between perceived risk and high online purchase intentions, however (Agudo-Peregrina, Acquila-Natale and Hernandez-Garcia, 2015).

From the literature review above, the following hypothesis is proposed:

H3: Age moderates the relationship between push motivation and online purchase intention.

H4: Age moderates the relationship between pull motivation and online purchase intention.

2.8 Conceptual Framework

To clarify, a conceptual framework will be used for this monograph with the guidance of a formal theory (Muhammad Dharma et al, 2019). The push and pull theory of motivation is used as the theoretical underpinning for the research (Mkubukeli and Cronje, 2018). This research aims to show that push factors and pull factors to be identified from research done here affect online purchase intentions (Mkubukeli and Cronje, 2018).

Literature reviewed in this monograph found that the relationship between independent variables and dependent variable can be determined by external factors in the case of push factors among the independent variables and by individual motives for the pull factors among the independent variables (Mkubukeli and Cronje, 2018). Push factors for online purchase intention are purchasing power, time saving, perceived risk and frequency of online purchases while pull factors for online purchase intention are trust, price comparison, advertising and brand name.

For this monograph, the moderating variable is age and it moderates the relationship between the independent variables and dependent variables.

The conceptual framework which governs this research is located below.

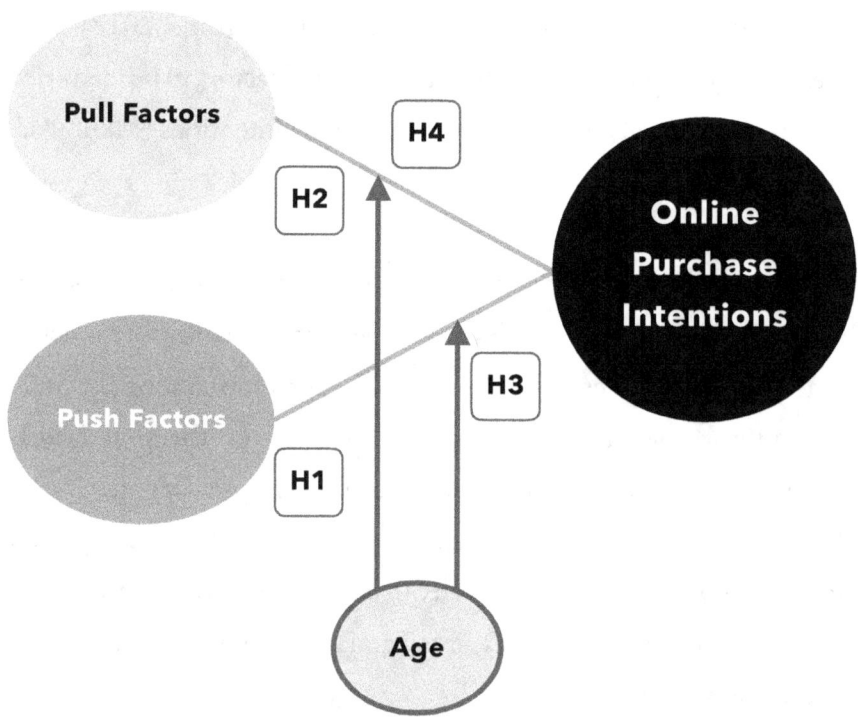

2.9 Summary

In conclusion, online purchase intentions are a shopper's willingness to purchase a product online and why or how much is the shopper willing to buy the aforementioned product online (Phang, Lee and Nabilah, 2019).

Online purchase intentions can be determined by the push factors of purchasing power (Chang and Chao, 2018), time saving (Kharel, 2018), perceived risk (Mazzini, Rohani and Salwana, 2016) and frequency of online purchases (Selvaraju and Karthikeyan, 2016) and the pull factors of trust (Hajli et al, 2017), price comparison (Khan, Liang and Shahzad, 2015), advertising (Ekpe, Adubasim and Adim, 2016) and brand name (Ghouri, ul Haq and Khan, 2017). Age will act as the moderating variable to determine its impact on the relationship between push factors and pull factors with the online purchase intentions of consumers (Liebana-Cabanillas and Alonso-Dos-Santos, 2017).

For the theoretical framework, the push and pull theory will be used as the theory guiding research for the monograph to look at the reasons behind the push factors and pull factors here (Mkubukeli and Cronje, 2018). Finally, a greater understanding of the questions and purposes of this research will be obtained from a conceptual framework (Muhammad Dharma et al, 2019).

Why Malaysian Consumers Prefer Online Purchases

CHAPTER 3

METHODOLOGY

3.0 Methodology

This chapter is about the research method to be used for this monograph and why it is needed.

Chapter 3: Methodology

3.1 Research Method

There are two categories of research methods to be used here, quantitative methods and qualitative methods (Creswell, 2014). Quantitative methods of research are based on numerical forms of data and includes a population and a sample (Creswell, 2014). Quantitative research looks at generalizable social behavioural aspects to product regularities with research for people's usage and amounts data which is collected and analysed (Rahman, 2017). Qualitative methods of research, in contrast, use text and image data, display uniqueness in data analysis and are based on different research designs (Creswell, 2014).

An advantage of choosing quantitative methods for research is that using quantitative methods in research can produce generalizable results (Shekhar et al, 2019), allowing quantitative methods in research to be used for research involving very large populations which may be difficult to reach for research purposes (Islam, 2018). Qualitative methods in research are advantageous in providing a detailed understanding of the subject to be researched (Shekhar et al, 2019) and use people's recorded words as its qualitative data to increase an understanding of people, the environments behind their lives and work and their motivations and actions (Myers, 2020). A disadvantage of using quantitative methods in research is that quantitative research minimizes organizations' social and cultural aspects when quantitative methods of research are used, but the ability to generalize the sample used here to a larger population makes the usage of quantitative methods in research more useful (Myers, 2020).

The research method to be chosen will use a quantitative method, or with a survey to be more precise (Creswell, 2014). This method of research would use questionnaires for data collection to assist in generalizing results from the sample answering these questionnaires to the sample's population (Creswell, 2014). Survey research allows a numeric or quantitative description of the population's trends when the research was done for this project and is done for this monograph, opinions or attitudes through studying a sample of this population (Creswell, 2014). This means creating survey questionnaires about factors affecting online purchase intentions and giving them to a sample of consumers in Malaysia, making a quantitative and numeric analysis based on studying the sample's responses and attitudes (the data collected) and creating a description which generalizes from the respondent sample to the population of the research done for the project (Creswell, 2014). For the research method, it is suggested that respondents for research done here be selected with convenience sampling and stratification of the population before determining the monograph's sample size to eliminate systematic bias in using survey participant characteristics to determine survey participants for answering the survey (Creswell, 2014).

Chapter 3: Methodology

The survey research to be used for this monograph will use variables and the identification of these variables' collective strength to test objective theories, besides true experiments (Creswell, 2014). With the survey research method to be used for this project, generalization and replication of this monograph's findings, suggestions for the deductive testing of theories, provisions to prevent research bias and controls for alternative explanations are expected (Creswell, 2014). As the quantitative research design used is non-experimental, a correlational design with the measurement and description of the relationship between variables used or obtained scores for the research done for this monograph as generated by the usage of the correlational statistic will be selected as the type of quantitative research design for this monograph (Creswell, 2014). With this research design used, it is possible to construct more complex relationships among variables used in the monograph (Creswell, 2014).

3.2 Research Design

———

For this monograph's research design, first, a survey questionnaire would be created based on the literature review cited. Then, the survey questionnaire would be reviewed and amended for approval based on feedback. This would be followed by distributing the survey questionnaire through hardcopy to respondents all across Malaysia. The specific venue was not specified, although the questionnaire's questions would be answered by hand after physically distributing the questionnaire's hardcopies (Phang, Lee and Nabilah, 2019). Therefore, it was not suggested that respondents answer the questionnaire within controlled settings (Phang, Lee and Nabilah, 2019).

After developing the questionnaire's questions and distributing the questionnaire to respondents, all respondents to the questionnaire answered the same set of questions from the questionnaire as this ensured validity in answers to these questions and to collect responses from these respondents efficiently before conducting a quantitative analysis of these responses (Zoha et al, 2017). After collecting several responses, the research questions for the monograph's questionnaire and their responses (results) were evaluated for their validity and based on respondent comments with a pilot test (Zoha et al, 2017). Then, new responses would be collected based on the validity of research questions and their results, depending on the need to amend the research questions based on the results collected (Zoha et al,

2017). As the minimum sample size for the project before it was converted into this monograph was 384 respondents, at least 384 valid respondents provided valid responses to be collected for this project's questionnaire's research questions from all across Malaysia before discussing these responses (results) to the research questions (Laub, 2019).

In the project's research design, push factors (purchasing power, time saving, perceived risk and frequency of online purchases) and pull factors (trust, price comparison, advertising, brand name) will form the independent variables, online purchase intentions will form the dependent variable and age will act as the moderating variable affecting the relationship between the independent variables and the dependent variable in this research (Creswell, 2014). The questionnaire will use the survey design to obtain and organize data for study in this monograph (Creswell, 2014). In addition, the survey design used for research collected data in a longitudinal manner over the time period of January 2020 to February 2020 (Creswell, 2014).

3.3 Questionnaire Development

———

The questionnaire's sections will be comprised of a brief introduction to the questionnaire for the first part, activities of the respondents for the second part, questions about how the push factors of respondents affect these respondents' online purchase intentions and questions about how the pull factors of respondents affect these respondents' online purchase intentions for the third part and information about the respondents for the fourth part.

A Likert Scale will be used for generating the answers to the questions in the questionnaire's second part, with "very strongly agree" being 1 and "very strongly disagree" (Moslehpour et al, 2016) being 7 (Joshi et al, 2015). Materials to be used for the questionnaire consist of paper (for hardcopy distribution).

Chapter 3: Methodology

3.4 Sampling Method

―――

Population is the total people in Malaysia, which was estimated to be 31,949,777 people in 2019, as quoted from Worldometers in 2020 (Worldometers, 2020). Given the population of 31,949,777, which was above 100,000, the sample size will be set as 384 people, using the Krejcie and Morgan Table which suggests that populations of 100,000 or more people should have a sample size of 384 people (Ndie, Anene and Ezenduka, 2019).

The reason why a sample size is required from a population to be questioned for research purposes is because it is impractical to ask every member of a research project's population as this will involve too many people, therefore, getting the right sample size with as few errors as possible for generalization purposes is needed (Islam, 2018). The sample size to be used for research purposes is based on the valid sample size (in number) of people from a research project's population to be selected to allow valid statistical inferences to be made from the population (Islam, 2018). The sample size of the population will be derived from nonprobability sampling, or more precisely, with convenience sampling (Creswell, 2014).

Convenience sampling, by definition, is a form of nonprobability sampling which involves target population members in sampling for a study due to the meeting of specific criteria by these members

(Etikan, Musa and Alkassim, 2016). The usage of convenience sampling has the issues of biased sampling and outliers affecting the reliability of using convenience sampling for this study in this paragraph (Etikan, Musa and Alkassim, 2016). Nevertheless, convenience sampling is chosen by this study due to the large population (31,949,777 people) and sample size (384 people) involved in the study and the issues of accessibility, limited time and limited resources while being more suited for quantitative research and generalisability to be used for this project's research than purposive sampling, another nonprobability sampling method (Etikan, Musa and Alkassim, 2016).

Table 3.1: Krejcie and Morgan Table for appropriate sample sizes based on population for research activities (Laub, 2019).

TOTAL	SAMPLE	TOTAL	SAMPLE	TOTAL	SAMPLE
10 ⇒	10	220 ⇒	140	1,200 ⇒	291
15 ⇒	14	230 ⇒	144	1,300 ⇒	297
20 ⇒	19	240 ⇒	148	1,400 ⇒	302
25 ⇒	24	250 ⇒	152	1,500 ⇒	306
30 ⇒	28	260 ⇒	155	1,600 ⇒	310
35 ⇒	32	270 ⇒	159	1,700 ⇒	313
40 ⇒	36	280 ⇒	162	1,800 ⇒	317
45 ⇒	40	290 ⇒	165	1,900 ⇒	320
50 ⇒	44	300 ⇒	169	2,000 ⇒	322
55 ⇒	48	320 ⇒	175	2,200 ⇒	327
60 ⇒	52	340 ⇒	181	2,400 ⇒	331
65 ⇒	56	360 ⇒	186	2,600 ⇒	335
70 ⇒	59	380 ⇒	191	2,800 ⇒	338
75 ⇒	63	400 ⇒	196	3,000 ⇒	341
80 ⇒	66	420 ⇒	201	3,500 ⇒	346
85 ⇒	70	440 ⇒	205	4,000 ⇒	351
90 ⇒	73	460 ⇒	210	4,500 ⇒	354
95 ⇒	76	480 ⇒	214	5,000 ⇒	357
100 ⇒	80	500 ⇒	217	6,000 ⇒	361
110 ⇒	86	550 ⇒	226	7,000 ⇒	364
120 ⇒	92	600 ⇒	234	8,000 ⇒	367
130 ⇒	97	650 ⇒	242	9,000 ⇒	368
140 ⇒	103	700 ⇒	248	10,000 ⇒	370
150 ⇒	108	750 ⇒	254	15,000 ⇒	375
160 ⇒	113	800 ⇒	260	20,000 ⇒	377
170 ⇒	118	850 ⇒	265	30,000 ⇒	379
180 ⇒	123	900 ⇒	269	40,000 ⇒	380
190 ⇒	127	950 ⇒	274	50,000 ⇒	381
200 ⇒	132	1,000 ⇒	278	75,000 ⇒	382
210 ⇒	136	1,100 ⇒	285	100,000 ⇒	384

3.5 Data Collection

It is expected that a confidence interval of +/- 4% (Creswell, 2014) and a 95% confidence coefficient of the interval will be used for research on respondent answers (Creswell, 2014), which means that for this research, there is a 95% probability that the parameter for the research is included in the confidence interval and the lower and upper limits for the confidence interval are likely to be the parameter's lower and upper bounds (Morey et al, 2016). In addition, the overall reliability of responses to a research question will be judged by using Cronbach's Alpha, with a recommended minimum threshold for the reliability of a research question's response being above 0.70 (Taber, 2018).

For this project, the data will be collected from people throughout Malaysia with nonprobability sampling (convenience sampling to be more precise) and a survey questionnaire (Creswell, 2014), given that this project's objective is to study the drivers affecting online purchase intention in Malaysia. It is planned that the data will be collected by hardcopy, given the sample size of 384 people (Laub, 2019) and the need to check for the reliability of responses and respondents while discarding invalid responses (Zoha et al, 2017), although hardcopies of the survey questionnaire will be distributed physically. The data will be collected from January 2020 to February 2020 throughout Malaysia. To investigate the relationship between push factors and pull factors affecting consumer online purchase intentions in Malaysia with their effects on consumer online purchase intentions in Malaysia for this research (Mkubukeli and Cronje, 2018) and the moderating impact of age on this relationship (Liebana-Cabanillas and Alonso-Dos-Santos, 2017), the procedure of collecting data and analysing survey results for this project will use a quantitative approach (Zoha et al, 2017).

3.6 Data Analysis

———

SPSS Analysis will be used for this project as it was used to facilitate a statistical analysis of the respondents' responses (data) (Cronk, 2018) by providing plenty of information (Stehlik-Barry and Babinec, 2017). The statistics to be entered for SPSS Analysis presentation in this research will be correlational statistics, as correlational statistics are based on relationships between variables and the relationships' strengths (Elliott and Woodward, 2016) and this research intends to evaluate the relationships between its push factors and its pull factors (independent variables) with the online purchase intentions of its respondents (dependent variable), besides how age (the moderating variable) affects the strength of these relationships. Therefore, correlational statistics are used to assist in evaluating the relationships between the project's independent variables and dependent variable (Elliott and Woodward, 2016) besides the relationships' strength and how it is affected by the project's moderating variable with the addition of a multiple regression model for a linear regression term (Laerd Statistics, 2018).

Multiple regression will be used for determining and analysing data from relationships attained from research for this project as it statistically defines the relationship between two or more independent variables and a single dependent variable (Jeon, 2015). More precisely, linear regression for continuously dependent variables will be used in this research (Jeon, 2015). Multiple regression will be determined for the research based on the relationship of association for these used variables with relative prediction of one variable within many variables in the research's outcome done in research for this project (Creswell, 2014). The multiple regression model (Laerd Statistics, 2018) will be used for multiple regression analysis (Anghelache, Manole and Anghel, 2015), which will be used to test hypothesis for this project's research (Bayer, Fachruddin and Torong, 2018). It is expected that with multiple regression analysis, an analysis of variance will be produced to generate an approximate percentage of the independent variables' (predictors') account for the dependent variable (criterion) of the research (Jeon, 2015). It must be noted that a problem with using the multiple regression analysis is the presence of multicollinearity, however, there has been discussion that multicollinearity in the usage of the multiple regression analysis for research is the result of interpreting high correlations between independent variables and interaction tools wrongly (Disatnik and Sivan, 2016).

Descriptive analysis will also be done to provide data analysis and a better understanding of the results generated from the data collected for this project's survey questionnaire when researched with the usage of description to clarify the results generated from the data (Ng, Chong and Mohmad, 2017). The descriptive analysis will look at the extent (Nurul et al, 2016) in which push factors and pull factors in this project's research (Mkubukeli and Cronje, 2018) affect online purchase intention of the respondents (Phang, Lee and Nabilah, 2019) and the extent in which age moderates the relationship between push factors and pull factors in this project's research with online purchase intention (Liebana-Cabanillas and Alonso-Dos-Santos, 2017). Descriptive analysis done on the research will be done with descriptive statistics by calculating the respective standard deviation and mean values for all variables involved in this project's research to obtain and facilitate an understanding of observed results for this study (Nurul et al, 2016).

For measurement of responses obtained from this project's research in the form of a questionnaire, the seven-point Likert Scale will be used (Joshi et al, 2015). This is to assist with understanding the opinions of respondents to questions in the project's questionnaires and surveys (Joshi et al, 2015). As opposed to a five-point Likert Scale, a seven-point Likert Scale is more accurate in looking at the opinions of respondents by providing more options which more accurately reflect the viewpoints of these respondents on the subject to be investigated in the report with less ambiguity (Joshi et al, 2015). It is intended that the Likert Scale be used in an 'interval scale' by combining all items answered by a single respondent to produce a single composite score for an individual with a realistic distance from another respondent's summative score to produce realistic 'interval estimates' for Likert Scale scores in this project (Joshi et al, 2015).

3.6.1 Pilot Test

Table 3.2: Pilot Test Table for the Cronbach's Alpha and Cronbach's Alpha Based on Standardized Items values for all variables of this project's research.

Type of Variable	Cronbach's Alpha	Cronbach's Alpha Based on Standardized Items	N of Items	Total Respondents
Push Factors	0.926	0.928	13	50
Pull Factors	0.923	0.925	14	50
Online Purchase Intention	0.867	0.869	4	50

An approved pilot test (Zoha et al, 2017) has also been done on the variables involved in the responses to this questionnaire used in this project's research (Lim et al, 2015). For the first portion of the pilot test, which was done over an hour on 5 February 2020, 50 responses were analysed with SPSS Analysis for push factors, pull factors and online purchase intention (Lim et al, 2015). The Cronbach's Alpha test for push factors produced a Cronbach's Alpha value of 0.926 and a Cronbach's Alpha Based on Standardized Items value of 0.928 for 13 questions (items), showing the high reliability of this questionnaire's responses based on the pilot test for push factors. The Cronbach's Alpha test for pull factors produced a Cronbach's Alpha value of 0.923 and a Cronbach's Alpha Based on Standardized Items value of 0.925 for 14 questions (items), showing the high reliability of this questionnaire's responses based on the pilot test for pull factors. The Cronbach's Alpha test for online purchase intention produced a Cronbach's Alpha value of 0.867 and a Cronbach's Alpha Based on Standardized Items value of 0.869 for 4 questions (items), showing the high reliability of this questionnaire's responses based on the pilot test for online purchase intention. It must be noted that scores above 0.80 in pilot tests, which are found in all scores derived from the project's pilot tests, prove these pilot tests' reliability (Lim et al, 2015). The questions used in and constructed for the pilot test have not been altered for the subsequent questionnaires distributed (Lim et al, 2015).

3.7 Summary

In conclusion, the project will use quantitative methods of research for its research methodology (Creswell, 2014) to obtain generalizable results (Shekhar et al, 2019). This is to assist with research dealing with large populations (Islam, 2018). Research will be done with a survey questionnaire about factors affecting online purchase intentions and giving the questionnaire to a sample of consumers in Malaysia, making a quantitative and numeric analysis by studying the responses and attitudes of the sample and creating a description which generalizes from the respondent sample to the population of the research (Creswell, 2014).

The research design for this project's survey questionnaire will involve hardcopy distribution to collect data for research (Creswell, 2014). For the questionnaire, its sample size is 384 respondents at minimum (Laub, 2019). A +/- 4% confidence interval will be expected from respondent answers for this questionnaire's research questions (Creswell, 2014). 0.70 is the minimum threshold to be used for reliability in measuring research question responses with Cronbach's Alpha (Taber, 2018).

Data analysis for this research will be done with SPSS Analysis for obtaining a statistical analysis of data collected for research, the responses of respondents to research done on this project (Cronk,

2018). To evaluate the relationships between the research's independent variables and dependent variable, correlational statistics will be used in the research for this project (Elliott and Woodward, 2016). For data analysis from the research's analysis, multiple regression will be used in the form of linear regression (Jeon, 2015). To provide an improved understanding of the results generated from the data collected for this project's survey questionnaire and to conduct data analysis, descriptive analysis will be used (Nurul et al, 2016). Finally, the seven-point Likert Scale will be used to measure responses to the project's survey questionnaire and identify the opinions of its respondents (Joshi et al, 2015).

CHAPTER 4

RESULTS

4.0 Results

―――――

This segment of the monograph analyses the impact of the push factors and the impact of the pull factors on the online purchase intentions of the project's interviewees as previously researched (Mkubukeli and Cronje, 2018).

The total number of respondents generated for this project's sample size is 424 respondents, which is a larger number of responses than the original intended target of 384 responses (Laub, 2019). The responses from only these 424 respondents can be used for this analysis, but it must be noted that at least 429 respondents have been interviewed for this project, however, at least 5 respondents have incomplete results which have been excluded from the analysis or did not answer, therefore a total response rate of 99% of respondents at maximum who answered the project's questions completely can be generated (Grundmann et al, 2017; Phang, Lee and Nabilah, 2019).

Before analysis, data has been evaluated to ensure that the data is entered and coded accurately (Phang, Lee and Nabilah, 2019). With the likelihood of random variation of data in mind, outliers have not been excluded from this analysis (Phang, Lee and Nabilah, 2019).

4.1.1 Demographics of the respondents

Table 4.1.1: Table for the gender of the respondents.

Gender	Number of Respondents
Female	210
Male	214

Table 4.1.2: Table for the ethnicity of the respondents.

Ethnicity	Number of Respondents
Chinese	264
Malay	66
Indian	37
Other	57

Table 4.1.3: Table for the employment level of the respondents.

Employment	Number of Respondents
Students	346
Private Sector	44
Self-employed / Business / Other Organization Owners	12
Unemployed, Homemakers, Housewives, or Retirees	14
Public Sector	8
Students	346

Based on the data generated for the survey used for this project's research, the total number of people who responded to the survey consists of 210 females and 214 males, which suggests that there are slightly more males than females who answered this survey, but a roughly equal number of male and female respondents otherwise (see Table 4.1.1 and Appendix E, pp. 233).

Based on ethnicity, the largest group of respondents are of Chinese ethnicity, with 264 respondents of Chinese ethnicity. This is followed by (in decreasing number of respondents by ethnicity) 66 ethnic

Chapter 4: Results

Malay respondents, 57 respondents of other ethnicities and 37 ethnic Indian respondents (see Table 4.1.2 and Appendix E, pp. 233).

With regard to employment, 346 of the respondents are students, making students the largest group of employment for this survey by a much higher number of respondents than those 44 respondents employed in the private sector, 12 employed as self-employed / business / other organization owners, 14 who are either unemployed, homemakers, housewives, or retirees in employment and 8 respondents employed in the public sector (see Table 4.1.3 and Appendix E, pp. 233).

Table 4.1.4: Table for the highest education level of the respondents.

Education Level	Number of Respondents
Bachelor's Degree	192
STPM / Foundation Studies / College Diploma / Professional Course / Vocational Studies	178
SPM or lower educational qualifications	42
Master's Degree or higher educational qualifications	12

Table 4.1.5: Table for the age groups of the respondents.

Age Group	Number of Respondents
Below 13 years of age	1
13 to 20 years of age	172
21 to 40 years of age	242
41 to 50 years of age	2
51 to 70 years of age	7
More than 70 years of age	0

Table 4.1.6: Table for the income per month of the respondents.

Income (RM)	Number of Respondents
Less than 3,000	354
3,000 to 5,000	32
5,000 and 10,000	21
10,000 or higher	17

Chapter 4: Results

For highest education level, more (192) respondents have Bachelor's Degree as their highest education level than STPM / Foundation Studies / College Diploma/ Professional Course / Vocational Studies with 178 respondents, SPM or lower educational qualifications with 42 respondents and Master's Degree or higher educational qualifications with 12 respondents (see Table 4.1.4 and Appendix E, pp. 233).

Most (242) respondents to this survey are aged 21 to 40 years, followed by 172 respondents aged 13 to 20 years, 7 respondents aged 51 to 70 years, 2 respondents aged 41 to 50 years, 1 respondent below 13 years of age, and no respondents older than 70 years of age (see Table 4.1.5 and Appendix E, pp. 233).

Finally, in income per month, most (354) respondents have an income per month of less than RM3,000, followed by an income per month of RM3,000 to RM5,000 for 32 respondents, an income per month of between RM5,000 to RM10,000 for 21 respondents and an income per month of between RM10,000 or higher for 17 respondents (see Table 4.1.6 and Appendix E, pp. 233).

4.1.2 Descriptive Analysis

───

This section discusses the descriptive analysis produced for the variables' items (Joshi et al, 2015) in the monograph with the descriptive statistics of mean and standard deviation (Nurul et al, 2016).

For the push factors variable, all thirteen push factor questions asked have generated means between 3.00 and 3.50 and standard deviations between 1.400 and 1.800 (see Table 4.1.7 and Appendix C, pp. 201). For the pull factors variable, the data collected for the fourteen pull factor questions have means between 2.50 and 3.70 and standard deviations between 1.400 and 1.900 (see Table 4.1.8 and Appendix C, pp. 201).

Finally, for the online purchase intentions, the data collected for all online purchase intention questions have means between 3.20 and 3.30 and standard deviations between 1.400 and 1.700 (see Table 4.1.9 and Appendix C, pp. 201).

Table 4.1.7: Table for the means and standard deviations of push factor questions.

Push Factor Question	Mean	Standard Deviation
H1	3.10	1.524
H2	3.31	1.508
H3	3.37	1.433
H4	3.21	1.730
H5	3.25	1.714
H6	3.17	1.680
H7	3.36	1.567
H8	3.18	1.618
H9	3.08	1.588
H10	3.22	1.464
H11	3.24	1.415
H12	3.36	1.533
H13	3.30	1.514

Table 4.1.8: Table for the means and standard deviations of pull factor questions.

Pull Factor Question	Mean	Standard Deviation
I1	3.24	1.557
I2	2.98	1.595
I3	2.95	1.745
I4	3.04	1.636
I5	2.92	1.885
I6	3.10	1.814
I7	3.24	1.649
I8	3.30	1.461
I9	3.41	1.497
I10	3.42	1.445
I11	3.60	1.656
I12	3.24	1.594
I13	3.31	1.605
I14	3.33	1.641

Table 4.1.9: Table for the means and standard deviations of online purchase intention questions.

Online Purchase Intention	Mean	Standard Deviation
L1	3.25	1.466
L2	3.27	1.563
L3	3.26	1.602
L4	3.27	1.580

The results above suggest that the figures for mean and standard deviation are smaller for the online purchase intention variable's items than the push factors variable's items and the pull factors variable's items (Nurul et al, 2016). The means seem to suggest that the respondents have 'slightly agree' as their attitude towards push factors and online purchase intention and 'strongly agree' or 'slightly agree' as their attitude towards pull factors with regard to online shopping (Nurul et al, 2016). In addition, the standard deviation values generated for the push factors variable's items, the pull factors variable's items and the online purchase intention variable's items suggest that these values are loosely clustered from the mean (Barcelona Field Studies Centre, 2020; Nurul et al, 2016).

It must be noted that the push factor questions variable has, among its items, 3.37 as its highest mean (generated by item H3) while the highest standard deviation is 1.730 (generated by item H4) (see Table 4.1.7 and Appendix C, pp. 201). For the pull factor questions variable, among its items, the highest mean is 3.60 (generated by item I11) while the highest standard deviation is 1.885 (generated by item I5) (see Table 4.1.8 and Appendix C, pp. 201). Finally, for online purchase intention, among its items, the highest mean is 3.27 (generated by items L2 and L4) while the highest standard deviation is 1.602 (generated by item L3) (see Table 4.1.9 and Appendix C, pp. 201). Therefore, the highest mean and highest standard deviation as generated from the pull factor questions variable are higher than the highest means and highest standard deviations for the push factor questions variable and the online purchase intention variable.

Table 4.1.10: Table for the mean and standard deviation of push factor variable.

Scale Statistics

Mean	Variance	Standard Deviation	Number of Items
42.15	209.733	14.482	13

Table 4.1.11: Table for the mean and standard deviation of pull factor variable.

Scale Statistics

Mean	Variance	Standard Deviation	Number of Items
45.06	285.682	16.902	14

Table 4.1.12: Table for the mean and standard deviation of online purchase intention variable.

Scale Statistics

Mean	Variance	Standard Deviation	Number of Items
13.05	28.954	5.381	4

Based on the results from Table 4.1.10, it can be said for the push factor variable that the variable's mean is 42.15 out of a possible range of means of the variable in scale ranging from between 13 to 91, which is slightly towards the lower end of the scale and suggests that the respondents slightly agree in attitude towards push factors, and the variable's standard deviation for all the variable's items is 14.482 (Yockey, 2016).

For the pull factor variable's results in Table 4.1.11, the mean is 45.06 out of a possible range of means of the variable in scale ranging from between 14 to 98, which is slightly towards the lower end of the scale and suggests that the respondents slightly agree in attitude towards pull factors, and the standard deviation for the variable based on all its items combined is 16.902 (Yockey, 2016).

Finally, from results obtained with Table 4.1.12, the mean for the online purchase intention variable is 13.05 out of a possible range of means of the variable in scale ranging from between 4 to 28, which is slightly towards the lower end of the scale and suggests that the respondents slightly agree in attitude towards online purchase intention, while the standard deviation for the online purchase intention variable based on all its items combined is 5.381 (Yockey, 2016).

The mean and standard deviation figures are smaller for the online purchase intention variable than the mean and standard deviation figures for the push factors variable and the pull factors variable, with all mean and standard deviation figures being collected with Scale Statistics generated from SPSS (Yockey, 2016). This is because of the smaller number of items in the online purchase intention variable compared to the number of items used in both the push factors variable and the pull factors variable (Yockey, 2016).

It must be noted that the mean, variance and standard deviation for Scale Statistics as generated from SPSS are the sum of the total scale (all items) for each variable used in this project's research (Yockey, 2016). Also, the scale standard deviation values generated for the push factors variable, the pull factors variable and the online purchase intention variable suggest that these standard deviation values are loosely clustered from the mean (Barcelona Field Studies Centre, 2020; Nurul et al, 2016).

4.2.1 Normality Tests for Push Factors, Pull Factors and Online Purchase Intention

―――

For the purpose of this normality test, skewness and kurtosis will be analysed (see Appendix C, pp. 201) as these values, if above 0, reveal deviations from the normal in distribution (Cain, Zhang and Yuan, 2017).

The skewness and kurtosis test will be first applied on push factors (Mkubukeli and Cronje, 2018; Cain, Zhang and Yuan, 2017). Upon analysis, it must be noted that all skewness and kurtosis values for all thirteen push factor questions fall between the acceptable ranges of -0.800 and 0.800 for skewness and -3.000 and 3.000 for kurtosis (see Table 4.2.1 and Appendix C, pp. 201) (Sook et al, 2017).

This analysis suggests the skewness and kurtosis values for push factors for this normality test are normal and within the accepted ranges for skewness and kurtosis values (Sook et al, 2017).

Table 4.2.1: Table for the skewness and kurtosis of push factor questions.

Push Factor Question	Value for Skewness	Value for Kurtosis
H1	0.481	-0.208
H2	0.424	-0.278
H3	0.323	-0.205
H4	0.553	-0.668
H5	0.525	-0.613
H6	0.530	-0.538
H7	0.370	-0.502
H8	0.466	-0.496
H9	0.512	-0.459
H10	0.428	-0.272
H11	0.433	-0.092
H12	0.383	-0.552
H13	0.419	-0.485

Next, the skewness and kurtosis for pull factors will be analysed with a normality test (Mkubukeli and Cronje, 2018; Cain, Zhang and Yuan, 2017).

Based on the analysed data below, all skewness and kurtosis values for all fourteen pull factor questions fall between the acceptable ranges of -0.800 and 0.800 for skewness and -3.000 and 3.000 for kurtosis (see Table 4.2.2 and Appendix C, pp. 201) (Sook et al, 2017).

This analysis suggests the values for skewness and kurtosis for pull factors in this normality test are normal and within the accepted ranges for skewness and kurtosis values (Sook et al, 2017).

Table 4.2.2: Table for the skewness and kurtosis of pull factor questions.

Pull factor question	Value for Skewness	Value for Kurtosis
I1	0.410	-0.429
I2	0.621	-0.210
I3	0.679	-0.522
I4	0.595	-0.411
I5	0.766	-0.548
I6	0.631	-0.601
I7	0.566	-0.424
I8	0.316	-0.322
I9	0.262	-0.411
I10	0.331	-0.324
I11	0.184	-0.743
I12	0.411	-0.471
I13	0.439	-0.477
I14	0.433	-0.491

Finally, skewness and kurtosis for online purchase intention will be analysed with a normality test (Phang, Lee and Nabilah, 2019; Cain, Zhang and Yuan, 2017).

From the analysed data, it can be stated that all skewness and kurtosis values for the four online purchase intention statements above are between the acceptable ranges of -0.800 and 0.800 for skewness and -3.000 and 3.000 for kurtosis (see Table 4.2.3 and Appendix C, pp. 201) (Sook et al, 2017). This means that the skewness and kurtosis values with regard to online purchase intention for this normality test are normal and within the accepted ranges for skewness and kurtosis values (Sook et al, 2017).

Table 4.2.3: Table for the skewness and kurtosis of online purchase intention questions.

Online Purchase Intention	Skewness	Kurtosis
L1	0.413	-0.327
L2	0.487	-0.474
L3	0.501	-0.505
L4	0.454	-0.442

4.2.2 Cronbach's Alpha tests

For testing the reliability of results obtained in this research, a Cronbach's Alpha test has been done with the 424 responses collected in research for this project using SPSS Analysis (Taber, 2018).

The Cronbach's Alpha value and the Cronbach's Alpha Based on Standardized Items value generated for push factors as a variable are both 0.919 for 13 questions (items) (see Table 4.2.4 and Appendix D, pp. 213). In contrast, for pull factors as a variable, the Cronbach's Alpha value generated for pull factors is 0.936 for 14 items and the Cronbach's Alpha Based on Standardized Items value for pull factors is 0.937 for 14 items (see Table 4.2.4 and Appendix D, pp. 213). Finally, online purchase intention as a variable has a Cronbach's Alpha value of 0.889 and a Cronbach's Alpha Based on Standardized Items value of 0.889 as well for 4 items (see Table 4.2.4 and Appendix D, pp. 213).

It must be noted that the push factors, pull factors and online purchase intention variables generated Cronbach's Alpha values above 0.70 (within the recommended threshold of acceptance), suggesting the reliability of results obtained in the research for this project with regard to push factors, pull factors and online purchase intention (Taber, 2018).

Table 4.2.4: Table for the Cronbach's Alpha and Cronbach's Alpha Based on Standardized Items values for all variables of this project.

Type of Variable	Cronbach's Alpha	Cronbach's Alpha Based on Standardized Items	N of Items	Total Respondents
Push Factors	0.919	0.919	13	424
Pull Factors	0.936	0.937	14	424
Online Purchase Intention	0.889	0.889	4	424

4.2.3 Multiple Regression Analysis

_____

This section analyses the multiple regression generated from the relationship between push factors with online purchase intention and pull factors with online purchase intention (Jeon, 2015).

Multiple regression analysis determines the strength of the relationship between an independent variable and a dependent variable (BMJ Publishing Group Ltd, 2020).

It must be noted that as the study tests push factors and pull factors as independent variables and online purchase intention as the dependent variable, the push factor questions and pull factor questions (items) have been combined to form the push factors variable and the pull factors variable respectively while online purchase intention statements (items) have been combined to form the online purchase intention variable (Hinton and McMurray, 2017).

Table 4.2.5: Table for collinearity statistics, 95% confidence intervals for B, R-value and R-square value for the relationship between push factors and online purchase intention.

Model	95.0% Confidence Interval for B Lower Bound	95.0% Confidence Interval for B Upper Bound	Collinearity Statistics Tolerance	Collinearity Statistics VIF	R-value	R-square value
Constant	0.397	0.998				
H14	0.704	0.880	1.000	1.000	0.655	0.429

With regard to the relationship between push factors with online purchase intention (Jeon, 2015), the collinearity statistics table has a Variance Inflation Factor of 1.000 and a tolerance of 1.000 as well, revealing a lack of multicollinearity through the Variance Inflation Factor as multicollinearity requires a Variance Inflation Factor above 5.00 (see Table 4.2.5 and Appendix D, pp. 213) (Kim, 2019). In addition, the R-square value, which determines the extent of variation of the dependent variable as affected by the independent variable (Finch, Bolin and Kelley, 2019), is 0.429, which shows moderate correlation between push factors acting as an independent variable and online purchase intention acting as a dependent variable (see Table 4.2.5 and Appendix D, pp. 213) (Insua, Frias and Perez Martinez, 2017; Mkubukeli and Cronje, 2018). There is a strong positive correlation between the independent (push factors) and dependent (online purchase intention) variables based on the R-value of 0.655 generated by the correlation's coefficient (BMJ Publishing Group Ltd, 2020), noting that the R-value of a correlation's coefficient reflects how strong the linear relationship between the independent and dependent variables is (see Table 4.2.5 and Appendix D, pp. 213) (Hazra and Gogtay, 2016). It must be noted that descriptive statistics have been included to support the multiple regression analysis for the relationship between push factors with online purchase intention and the relationship between pull factors with online purchase intention (Hart, 2018).

Table 4.2.6: Table for collinearity statistics, 95% confidence intervals for B, R-value and R-square value for the relationship between pull factors and online purchase intention.

Model	95.0% Confidence Interval for B Lower Bound	95.0% Confidence Interval for B Upper Bound	Collinearity Statistics Tolerance	Collinearity Statistics VIF	R-value	R-square value
Constant	0.221	0.675				
I15	0.809	0.941	1.000	1.000	0.785	0.616

In addition, the relationship between pull factors and online purchase intention will be analysed (Jeon, 2015). For the relationship between pull factors and online purchase intention, the collinearity statistics table has a Variance Inflation Factor of 1.000 and a tolerance of 1.000 as well, revealing a lack of multicollinearity through the Variance Inflation Factor as multicollinearity requires a Variance Inflation Factor above 5.00 (see Table 4.2.6 and Appendix D, pp. 213) (Kim, 2019). A strong correlation between the independent and dependent variables based on the R-value of 0.785 is generated by the correlation's coefficient (see Table 4.2.6 and Appendix D, pp. 213) (BMJ Publishing Group Ltd, 2020). In addition, the R-square value obtained for the relationship between pull factors and online purchase intention is 0.616, which shows strong correlation between pull factors acting as an independent variable and online purchase intention acting as a dependent variable (see Table 4.2.6 and Appendix D, pp. 213) (Insua, Frias and Perez Martinez, 2017; Mkubukeli and Cronje, 2018).

Table 4.2.7: Table for Unstandardized Coefficients, Standardized Coefficients, t-value and significance value for the relationship between push factors and online purchase intention.

Model	Unstandardized Coefficients B	Unstandardized Coefficients Standard Error	Standardized Coefficients Beta	t-value	Significance value
Constant	0.697	0.153		4.561	0.000
H14	0.792	0.045	0.655	17.780	0.000

In the relationship between push factors and online purchase intention, the significance values for the relationship's constant and relationship coefficients displayed are 0.000, which shows that this relationship is significant as its significance value is less than 0.05 (see Table 4.2.7 and Appendix D, pp. 213) (Zhu, 2016; UCLA, 2020a).

In addition, with regard to beta coefficients, which are used to evaluate the strengths of variables in this research comparatively, the beta coefficient of 17.780 in t-value for the relationship between push factors and online purchase intention and the t-value of 4.561 generated for the relationship's constant's beta coefficient show a significant difference from zero due to the significant beta coefficient produced by this relationship (see Table 4.2.7 and Appendix D, pp. 213) (Khan, Rehman and Rehman, 2013; Statistics Solutions, 2020; UCLA, 2020b). The beta coefficients of 17.780 and 4.561 (for the constant) in t-value as produced by the relationship between push factors and online purchase intention show that the relationship is significant because the beta coefficient values are above the minimum value of 2.00 needed to proof the relationship's significance (Eldenburg et al, 2020).

In addition, a beta coefficient of 0.655 has been obtained for push factors in the relationship between push factors and online purchase intention, showing that a standard deviation increase in push factors causes a 0.655 increase in standard deviation for online purchase intention in this relationship when other variables are constant (see Table 4.2.7 and Appendix D, pp. 213) (UCLA, 2020b).

Table 4.2.8: Table for Unstandardized Coefficients, Standardized Coefficients, t-value and significance value for the relationship between pull factors and online purchase intention.

Model	Unstandardized Coefficients B	Unstandardized Coefficients Standard Error	Standardized Coefficients Beta	t-value	Significance value
Constant	0.448	0.115		3.879	0.000
I15	0.875	0.034	0.785	26.043	0.000

As the relationship between pull factors and online purchase intention generated significance values of 0.000 based on the coefficients displayed for the relationship and the relationship's constant, with the significance values below 0.05, the relationship between pull factors and online purchase intention, based on significance value, is significant (see Table 4.2.8 and Appendix D, pp. 213) (Zhu, 2016; UCLA, 2020a). The beta coefficient of 26.043 in t-value as generated from the relationship between pull factors and online purchase intention and the beta coefficient t-value of 3.879 as obtained from the constant of the relationship between pull factors and online purchase intention are significant and reveal the relationship's significance as both beta coefficient t-values are above the minimum t-value of 2.00

to show a significant difference from zero in this relationship (see Table 4.2.8 and Appendix D, pp. 213) (Khan, Rehman and Rehman, 2013; Statistics Solutions, 2020; UCLA, 2020b; Eldenburg et al, 2020). Also, the relationship between pull factors and online purchase intention has generated a beta coefficient of 0.785, showing that a standard deviation increase in pull factors leads to a 0.785 increase in standard deviation for online purchase intention in this relationship when other variables are constant (see Table 4.2.8 and Appendix D, pp. 213) (UCLA, 2020b).

Table 4.2.9: Table for collinearity statistics, 95% confidence intervals for B, R-value and R-square value for the impact of age on the relationship between push factors and online purchase intention.

Model	95.0% Confidence Interval for B Lower Bound	95.0% Confidence Interval for B Upper Bound	Collinearity Statistics Tolerance	Collinearity Statistics VIF	R-value	R-square value
Constant	0.376	1.411				
H14	0.706	0.881	0.998	1.002	0.655	0.429
Age	-0.242	0.088	0.998	1.002	0.656	0.430

The multiple regression analysis on how age affects the relationship between push factors and online purchase intention will also be discussed in this monograph (Sharifi Fard et al, 2016). The impact of age on the relationship between push factors and online purchase intention has produced on the collinearity statistics table a Variance Inflation Factor of 1.002 and a tolerance of 0.998, revealing a lack of multicollinearity through the Variance Inflation Factor as multicollinearity requires a Variance Inflation Factor above 5.00 (see Table 4.2.9 and Appendix D, pp. 213) (Kim, 2019). The R-value for the correlation between the independent and dependent variables is 0.656 due to the impact of age, showing that the correlation is a strong correlation (BMJ Publishing Group Ltd, 2020). In contrast, the impact of age on the relationship between push factors and online purchase intention (see Table 4.2.9 and Appendix D, pp. 213) generated a R-square value of 0.430 (Finch, Bolin and Kelley, 2019), which suggests a moderate correlation based on R-square value (BMJ Publishing Group Ltd, 2020).

Table 4.2.10: Table for Unstandardized Coefficients, Standardized Coefficients, t-value and significance value for the impact of age on the relationship between push factors and online purchase intention.

Model	Unstandardized Coefficients B	Unstandardized Coefficients Standard Error	Standardized Coefficients Beta	t-value	Significance value
Constant	0.894	0.263		3.395	0.001
H14	0.794	0.045	0.656	17.800	0.000
Age	-0.077	0.084	-0.034	-0.916	0.360

Chapter 4: Results

For the impact of age on the relationship between push factors and online purchase intention, the beta coefficient of -0.916 in t-value generated from the impact of age for the age variable alone does not reveal a significant difference from zero because the beta coefficient generated from the age variable is below 2.00 in t-value and is not significant (see Table 4.2.10 and Appendix D, pp. 213) (Khan, Rehman and Rehman, 2013; Statistics Solutions, 2020; UCLA, 2020b; Eldenburg et al, 2020). However, the impact of age on the relationship between push factors and online purchase intention can be stated to have a significant difference from zero, with the impact of age on the relationship between push factors and online purchase intention generating a beta coefficient of 17.800 in t-value and a beta coefficient of 3.395 for the relationship's constant based on t-value (see Table 4.2.10 and Appendix D, pp. 213) (Khan, Rehman and Rehman, 2013; Statistics Solutions, 2020; UCLA, 2020b; Eldenburg et al, 2020).

In addition, the impact of age on the relationship between push factors and online purchase intention has also produced a beta coefficient value of 0.656, suggesting that a standard deviation increase in push factors leads to a 0.656 increase in standard deviation for online purchase intention when other variables are constant (UCLA, 2020b), and a standardized coefficient of -0.034 for the age variable, which means that every standard deviation increase on the age variable leads to a 0.034 decrease in standard deviation for the relationship between push factors and online purchase intention (see Table 4.2.10 and Appendix D, pp. 213) (UCLA, 2020b). Based on the relationship's displayed coefficients, the significance values generated by the role of age as a moderating variable on the relationship between push factors and online purchase intention are 0.000 for the relationship's coefficient and 0.001 for the relationship's constant coefficient, showing that age has a significant impact on the relationship between push factors and online purchase intention (see Table 4.2.10 and Appendix D, pp. 213) (Zhu, 2016; UCLA, 2020a). However, the significance value coefficient generated for age with regard to the moderating impact of age on the relationship between push factors and online purchase intention is 0.360, which is above 0.05 and suggests that age does not have a significant impact on the relationship between push factors and online purchase intention (see Table 4.2.10 and Appendix D, pp. 213) (Zhu, 2016; UCLA, 2020a).

Table 4.2.11: Table for collinearity statistics, 95% confidence intervals for B, R-value and R-square value for the impact of age on the relationship between pull factors and online purchase intention.

Model	95.0% Confidence Interval for B Lower Bound	95.0% Confidence Interval for B Upper Bound	Collinearity Statistics Tolerance	Collinearity Statistics VIF	R-value	R-square value
Constant	0.311	1.136				
I15	0.811	0.943	0.998	1.002	0.785	0.616
Age	-0.243	0.027	0.998	1.002	0.787	0.619

From how the relationship between pull factors and online purchase intention will be affected by age (Sharifi Fard et al, 2016), based on multiple regression analysis, the collinearity statistics table's Variance Inflation Factor value of 1.002 and tolerance value of 0.998, reveal a lack of multicollinearity through the Variance Inflation Factor as multicollinearity requires a Variance Inflation Factor above 5.00 (see Table 4.2.11 and Appendix D, pp. 213) (Kim, 2019).

For the correlation between pull factors and online purchase intention as affected by age, the analysis for this correlation generated a R-value of 0.787, showing strong correlation (see Table 4.2.11 and Appendix D, pp. 213) (BMJ Publishing Group Ltd, 2020).

Based on R-square value (Finch, Bolin and Kelley, 2019), the impact of age on the relationship between pull factors and online purchase intention also suggests a strong correlation between pull factors and online purchase intention when impacted by age, with a R-square value of 0.619 generated by this correlation (see Table 4.2.11 and Appendix D, pp. 213) (BMJ Publishing Group Ltd, 2020).

Table 4.2.12: Table for Unstandardized Coefficients, Standardized Coefficients, t-value and significance value for the impact of age on the relationship between push factors and online purchase intention.

Model	Unstandardized Coefficients B	Unstandardized Coefficients Standard Error	Standardized Coefficients Beta	t-value	Significance value
Constant	0.724	0.210		3.449	0.001
I15	0.877	0.034	0.787	26.134	0.000
Age	-0.108	0.069	-0.047	-1.574	0.116

With regard to the impact of age on the relationship between pull factors and online purchase intention, a significant difference from zero cannot be revealed by the beta coefficient of -1.574 in t-value generated from the impact of age through the age variable alone as the age variable's beta coefficient is smaller than the t-value of 2.00 needed for beta coefficient significance (see Table 4.2.12 and Appendix D, pp. 213) (Khan, Rehman and Rehman, 2013; Statistics Solutions, 2020; UCLA, 2020b; Eldenburg et al, 2020).

That said, a significant difference from zero can be obtained from the impact of age on the relationship between pull factors and online purchase intention, with the impact of age on the relationship between pull factors and online purchase intention generating a beta coefficient of 26.134 in t-value and a beta coefficient of 3.449 for the relationship's constant based on t-value (see Table 4.2.12 and Appendix D, pp. 213) (Khan, Rehman and Rehman, 2013; Statistics Solutions, 2020; Eldenburg et al, 2020; UCLA, 2020b).

Also, the beta coefficient value for the impact of age on the relationship between pull factors and online purchase intention is 0.787, suggesting that a standard deviation increase in pull factors leads to a 0.787 increase in standard deviation for online purchase intention when other variables are constant (UCLA, 2020b), and -0.047 for the age variable, which means that every standard deviation increase on the age variable leads to a 0.047 decrease in standard deviation for the relationship between pull factors and online purchase intention (see Table 4.2.12 and Appendix D, pp. 213) (UCLA, 2020b).

The significance values generated by the role of age as a moderating variable on the relationship between pull factors and online purchase intention are 0.001 based on the relationship's displayed constant coefficient and 0.000 for the relationship's coefficient respectively, showing that age has a significant impact on the relationship between pull factors and online purchase intention (see Table 4.2.12 and Appendix D, pp. 213) (Zhu, 2016; UCLA, 2020a).

The moderating variable of age, based on age's impact on the relationship between pull factors and online purchase intention generated a significance value coefficient of 0.116, which is above 0.05 and suggests that age does not have a significant impact on the relationship between pull factors and online purchase intention (see Table 4.2.12 and Appendix D, pp. 213) (Zhu, 2016; UCLA, 2020a).

4.3 Summary

From the results obtained above, the obtaining of this project's push factors (purchasing power, time saving, perceived risk and frequency of online purchases) which affect online purchase intention is supported by the push factors' items' skewness and kurtosis (Mkubukeli and Cronje, 2018; Sook et al, 2017). Similarly, the obtaining of this project's pull factors (trust, price comparison, advertising and brand name) which impact online purchase intention is proven by the pull factors' items' skewness and kurtosis (Mkubukeli and Cronje, 2018; Sook et al, 2017). In addition, all Cronbach's Alpha values for each of the items belonging to the push factors variable, the pull factors variable and the online purchase intention variable have been found to have values above 0.70, proving the reliability of the push factors and pull factors used in this monograph (Taber, 2018). Therefore, the research objective of finding the push factors and the pull factors which drive the online purchase intention for consumers in Malaysia (RO1) has been achieved by the results generated.

For the research objective of studying the effect of push factors on the online purchase intention of consumers in Malaysia (RO2), a strong positive correlation can be noticed in the relationship between push factors and online purchase intention based on R-value (BMJ Publishing Group Ltd, 2020) and a moderate positive correlation based on R-square value (Finch, Bolin and Kelley, 2019; Insua, Frias and

Perez Martinez, 2017). Also, the hypothesis that a positive relationship exists between push factors and online purchase intention (H1) can be supported based on the strong positive correlation generated by this relationship's R-value and the moderate positive correlation produced through this relationship's R-square value (Finch, Bolin and Kelley, 2019; Insua, Frias and Perez Martinez, 2017; BMJ Publishing Group Ltd, 2020). Therefore, with regard to the impact of push factors on the online purchase intention of consumers in Malaysia (RO2), push factors have been found to have a strong positive effect on online purchase intention.

With regard to the research objective of studying the effect of pull factors on the online purchase intention of consumers in Malaysia (RO3), a strong positive correlation has been generated in the relationship between pull factors and online purchase intention based on both R-value (BMJ Publishing Group Ltd, 2020) and R-square value (Finch, Bolin and Kelley, 2019; Insua, Frias and Perez Martinez, 2017). The R-value and R-square value obtained for the relationship between pull factors and online purchase intention, with the strong positive correlations generated by these values, support the hypothesis that a positive relationship between pull factors and online purchase intention exists (H2) (Finch, Bolin and Kelley, 2019; Insua, Frias and Perez Martinez, 2017; BMJ Publishing Group Ltd, 2020).

Therefore, it can be said that pull factors have been found to have a strong positive impact on online purchase intention in relation to the research objective of studying the effect of pull factors on the online purchase intention of consumers in Malaysia (RO3).

Finally, when the moderating effect of age on the relationship between motivation factors (push factors and pull factors) with the online purchase intention of consumers in Malaysia is analysed as a research objective (RO4), a strong correlation in R-value and a moderate correlation in R-square value have been generated from the usage of age as a moderating variable on the relationship between push factors and online purchase intention (Sharifi Fard et al, 2016; BMJ Publishing Group Ltd, 2020; Finch, Bolin and Kelley, 2019; Insua, Frias and Perez Martinez, 2017).

For the usage of age as a moderating variable on the relationship between pull factors and online purchase intention, a strong correlation in both R-value and R-square value respectively has been generated (Sharifi Fard et al, 2016; BMJ Publishing Group Ltd, 2020; Finch, Bolin and Kelley, 2019; Insua, Frias and Perez Martinez, 2017).

In addition, the hypothesis that age moderates the relationship between push factors and online purchase intention (H3) and the hypothesis that age moderates the relationship between pull factors and online purchase intention (H4) can be proven based on the positive correlations generated by both the impact of age on the relationship between push factors and online purchase intention and the impact of age on the relationship between pull factors and online purchase intention (BMJ Publishing Group Ltd, 2020; Insua, Frias and Perez Martinez, 2017; Finch, Bolin and Kelley, 2019).

In conclusion, when the moderating effect of age on the relationship between motivation factors (push factors and pull factors) with the online purchase intention of consumers in Malaysia is analysed as a research objective (RO4), age has a strong positive impact as a moderating variable on the relationship between motivation factors (push factors and pull factors) with online purchase intention of consumers in Malaysia (RO4).

CHAPTER 5

CONCLUSION

5.0 Conclusion

This chapter is about the conclusions reached for this research.

Chapter 5: Conclusion

5.1 Summary of analysis done on Research Objectives

———

5.1.1 Push Factors and Pull Factors

———

In relation to the project's first research objective, the determining of the push factors and pull factors driving online purchase intention among consumers in Malaysia (RO1), all push factor items and pull factor items have been found to have skewness and kurtosis within acceptable ranges of between -0.800 and 0.800 for skewness and between -3.000 and 3.000 for kurtosis (Sook et al, 2017). Therefore, all push factor items and pull factor items used for this project are suitable for usage as their skewness and kurtosis are within acceptable skewness and kurtosis ranges (Sook et al, 2017).

In addition, the Cronbach's Alpha values for the items in both the push factors variable and pull factors variable are all above 0.70, showing that the push factors and pull factors used for this research are reliable (Taber, 2018). The reliability shown by all push factors means that, as stated earlier, purchasing power, time saving, perceived risk and frequency of online purchases can be used and determined as push factors for the monograph (Lim, Azizah and Ramayah, 2015; Kharel, 2018; Mazzini, Rohani and Salwana, 2016; Kanchan, Kumar and Gupta, 2015; Mkubukeli and Cronje, 2018). In addition, based on the reliability of results generated by all pull factors, trust, price comparison, advertising and brand image can also be used and determined as pull factors for this research (Bulut, 2015; Khan, Liang and Shahzad, 2015; Ekpe, Adubasim and Adim, 2016; Faryabi, Fesaghandis and Saed, 2015; Mkubukeli and Cronje, 2018).

Chapter 5: Conclusion

5.1.2 Push factors and Online Purchase Intention

From the multiple regression analysis generated, and in relation to the research objective which aims to study the relationship between push factors and its driving of online purchase intention among consumers in Malaysia (RO2), the relationship between push factors and its driving of online purchase intention among consumers in Malaysia has been found to be strong and positive, having generated a strong positive R-value and a moderate positive R-square value (Finch, Bolin and Kelley, 2019; Insua, Frias and Perez Martinez, 2017; BMJ Publishing Group Ltd, 2020).

The relationship between push factors and online purchase intention has also been discovered not to be compromised by multicollinearity (Kim, 2019). This supports the studies which suggests that push factors (purchasing power, time saving, perceived risk and frequency of online purchases) have a significant impact on online purchase intention (Li and Hou, 2019; Rrumbullaku and Kume, 2017; Mazzini, Rohani and Salwana, 2016; Kanchan, Kumar and Gupta, 2015; Mkubukeli and Cronje, 2018). Also, it must be noted that the generated results for R-value and R-square value for the relationship between push factors and online purchase intention support the H1 hypothesis that push factors positively influence online purchase intention (Finch, Bolin and Kelley, 2019; Insua, Frias and Perez Martinez, 2017; BMJ Publishing Group Ltd, 2020).

Push factors force action from people through external factors (Mkubukeli and Cronje, 2018). Purchasing power can be used as a push factor for this research through the higher income levels needed for a person to increase his online purchase intentions (Lim, Azizah and Ramayah, 2015; Li and Hou, 2019; Irianto, 2015).

In addition, higher purchasing power can influence online purchase intention by affecting the bargaining power of customers who shop online (Tseng et al, 2017). The validity of time saving as a push factor can be seen through the ability of online purchases to save time compared to other methods of purchases (Jadhav and Khanna, 2016). This is because online purchases allow purchases to be made from home, saving time otherwise spent travelling outside of home (Rrumbullaku and Kume, 2017).

With regard to perceived risk as a push factor, increased perceived risk increases the potential for negative opinions which affect online purchase intentions with uncertainty about serious outcomes occurring during an online purchase (Mazzini, Rohani and Salwana, 2016). In addition, perceived risk negatively affects online purchase intention because perceived risk can increase the customers' fears about buying the wrong products online (Ariffin, Mohan and Goh, 2018).

Finally, with regard to the validity as a push factor of frequency of online purchases, more frequent online purchases have been found to improve the intentions of customers to purchase things online

(Kanchan, Kumar and Gupta, 2015). This is because a higher frequency of online purchases among customers, through provided shopping experience, increases the customers' online purchase intention (Arulkumar and Kannaiah, 2015).

5.1.3 Pull factors and Online Purchase Intention

———

Through the usage of multiple regression analysis and in relation to the research objective that intends to evaluate how pull factors drive online purchase intention among consumers in Malaysia (RO3), the driving of online purchase intention among consumers in Malaysia by pull factors has a strong relationship, with a positive strong R-value and a positive strong R-square value respectively (Finch, Bolin and Kelley, 2019; Insua, Frias and Perez Martinez, 2017; BMJ Publishing Group Ltd, 2020). Also, multicollinearity has been found to be not present in the relationship between pull factors and online purchase intention (Kim, 2019). The values generated for the R-value and R–square value for the relationship between pull factors and online purchase intention support the H2 hypothesis that pull factors positively influence online purchase intention (Finch, Bolin and Kelley, 2019; Insua, Frias and Perez Martinez, 2017; BMJ Publishing Group Ltd, 2020). The studies which suggest that pull factors (trust, price comparison, advertising and brand image) have a significant impact on online purchase intention are therefore supported (Bulut, 2015; Khan, Liang and Shahzad, 2015; Ekpe, Adubasim and Adim, 2016; Ghouri, ul Haq and Khan, 2017; Mkubukeli and Cronje, 2018).

Pull factors encourage action from people with internal motivation and attraction (Mkubukeli and Cronje, 2018). Trust can be utilised as a pull factor for online purchase intention as trust determines the customer retention in online shopping needed to generate online purchase intentions given the recent developments in online shopping (Rezaei, Emami and Valaei, 2016). In addition, trust can also reduce uncertainties involved in online shopping (Bulut, 2015).

Price comparison can be proven to be a pull factor which affects online purchase intentions of customers as price comparison from online shopping allows customers to find lower priced products, improving these customers' online purchase intention (Khan, Liang and Shahzad, 2015). In addition, price comparison can determine perceived product quality, which also affects customers' online purchase intentions (Beranek, Remes and Nydl, 2017).

Advertising, through increasing exposure to products to be purchased with online shopping, can also be proven to affect online purchase intentions as a pull factor (Ekpe, Adubasim and Adim, 2016). Advertising also increases online purchase intentions of customers by creating brand images of advertised products (Kowang et al, 2019). Finally, through improving the perceived value and affordability of products to be purchased online, in addition to customer attitudes to the products' brand, brand name also acts as an effective pull factor for enhancing customers' online purchase intention (Faryabi, Fesaghandis and Saed, 2015; Mostafa and Elseidi, 2018).

5.1.4 The impact of age as the moderating variable on the relationship between Push Factors / Pull Factors and Online Purchase Intention

From the multiple regression analysis generated and the research objective of determining the moderating impact of age on the relationship between motivation (push and pull) factors and online purchase intention (RO4), the impact of age as a moderating variable on the relationship between push factors and online purchase intention has produced a positive strong R-value and a positive moderate R-square value respectively (Finch, Bolin and Kelley, 2019; Insua, Frias and Perez Martinez, 2017; BMJ Publishing Group Ltd, 2020). Multicollinearity has been found to not affect the role of age as a moderating variable to the relationship between push factors and online purchase intention (Kim, 2019).

In addition, the H3 hypothesis that age moderates the relationship between push factors and online purchase intention is proven by results obtained for the R-value and R–square value for how age impacts the relationship between push factors and online purchase intention (Finch, Bolin and Kelley, 2019; Insua, Frias and Perez Martinez, 2017; BMJ Publishing Group Ltd, 2020). The studies which suggest that age moderates the relationship between push factors and online purchase intention are therefore supported (Schurink, 2019; Li and Hou, 2019; Mkubukeli and Cronje, 2018).

Chapter 5: Conclusion

The role of age as a moderating variable on the relationship between pull factors and online purchase intention has been found to be not affected by multicollinearity (Kim, 2019). In addition, the positive strong R-value and positive strong R–square value obtained for how age affects the relationship between pull factors and online purchase intention strongly support the H4 hypothesis that age moderates the relationship between pull factors and online purchase intention (Finch, Bolin and Kelley, 2019; Insua, Frias and Perez Martinez, 2017; BMJ Publishing Group Ltd, 2020). Therefore, research which suggests that age moderates the relationship between pull factors and online purchase intention is supported (Schurink, 2019; Li and Hou, 2019; Mkubukeli and Cronje, 2018).

The belief that age moderates the relationship between push factors and pull factors with online purchase intention can be further supported by reviewed literature (Liebana-Cabanillas and Alonso-Dos-Santos, 2017). This is because age controls online purchase intention by defining familiarity with online activities (Schurink, 2019).

In addition, age also acts as a moderating variable to online purchase intention by determining the higher initiative of younger people to save money, with this initiative subsequently leading to higher online purchase intentions among younger people (Li and Hou, 2019). This is in addition to age acting as a moderating variable for online purchase intentions among customers through determining the customers' mental accounts (Li and Hou, 2019). Therefore, age can be determined as a moderating variable for the relationship between push factors and pull factors with online purchase intention (Li and Hou, 2019).

Chapter 5: Conclusion

5.2 Significance of the Study

―――――

The purpose and significance of the study is to fill the gap in literature caused by the lack of recent literature done on how push factors and pull factors affect online purchase intention in the Malaysian context (Fatin, Noor and Kalsitinoor, 2019). It must be noted that this piece of research is done in the Malaysian context and therefore, takes into consideration the values of Malaysians (Phang, Lee and Nabilah, 2019).

In addition, it is expected that the study is useful for assisting businesses in modifying their operations and surveyed consumers across Malaysia in modifying their habits to encourage online purchases and online purchase intention across Malaysia (in percentage of Malaysia's population and number of online shoppers) in the future, preferably to maximise online purchases in Malaysia until most people (especially most adults) in Malaysia conduct purchases online (Phang, Lee and Nabilah, 2019).

5.3 Limitations

———

An example of limitations to be dealt with was time constraints since this research was based on a project which was done in 37 weeks (including school holidays). This restricted the amount of time in which research could be properly done for the project, especially for conducting questionnaires about online purchase intentions in Malaysia. The time limitation had been treated seriously given the needed minimum sample size of 384 students to be questioned and the hours of time needed to interview students for the project in addition to the huge amount of research needed for the project version of this monograph and other activities (Laub, 2019).

Also, information not collected by respondent demographics but which may be relevant in the Malaysian context such as state may be collected and used for future research (Phang, Lee and Nabilah, 2019). In this situation, it is suggested that only respondents living in Malaysian states other than the states of this research's respondents be interviewed to avoid bias in collected data and results to future research (Phang, Lee and Nabilah, 2019). It is suggested that future research be done which looks at how the specific Malaysian state of residence for research respondents affects their intention to purchase things online, either as an independent variable or a dependent variable (Phang, Lee and Nabilah, 2019).

5.4 Recommendations

———

It is recommended that this monograph be used by Malaysian businesses to change their operations by increasing online purchases and online purchase intentions across Malaysia (in percentage of Malaysia's population and number of online shoppers) (Phang, Lee and Nabilah, 2019). This is to allow Malaysian businesses to catch up with the increasing importance (Arshad, Ibrahim and Chook, 2016) and profitability of providing online shopping to their customers (The Star, 2019).

In addition, it is recommended that this monograph is read by Malaysian consumers to encourage them to shop online with recognition of the factors which determine online purchase intention (Phang, Lee and Nabilah, 2019).

Finally, it is recommended that research on factors affecting online purchases in national settings not previously researched in online purchase intention studies increases in the future (Phang, Lee and Nabilah, 2019).

5.5 Conclusion

In conclusion, the research has accomplished the objectives of studying the impact of push factors and pull factors (Mkubukeli and Cronje, 2018) on the online purchase intention of the project's respondents in Malaysia (Mohd Fawzy et al, 2018).

The results obtained found that push factors and pull factors (Mkubukeli and Cronje, 2018) can be proven to have a positive relationship in impact with the online purchase intention of customers in Malaysia (Mohd Fawzy et al, 2018) based on R-square values (Finch, Bolin and Kelley, 2019; Insua, Frias and Perez Martinez, 2017) and R-values generated by this relationship (BMJ Publishing Group Ltd, 2020).

This means that push factors and pull factors (Mkubukeli and Cronje, 2018) determine the online purchase intention of customers in Malaysia (Mohd Fawzy et al, 2018).

In addition, based on R-square values and R-values generated, it has been found that age can be proven to act as a moderating variable to the relationship between push factors and online purchase intention and the relationship between pull factors and online purchase intention (Finch, Bolin and Kelley, 2019;

Chapter 5: Conclusion

Insua, Frias and Perez Martinez, 2017; BMJ Publishing Group Ltd, 2020).

Therefore, age acts as a moderating variable to both the relationship between push factors and online purchase intention and the relationship between pull factors and online purchase intention (Schurink, 2019; Li and Hou, 2019; Mkubukeli and Cronje, 2018).

Why Malaysian Consumers Prefer Online Purchases

REFERENCES

Abdul Kadir, O., Lailatul Faizah, A. H., Muhammad Iskandar, H., Amirun, R. R., Mohamad Amir, S. S., Mohd Safwan, R., Muhammad Amir, O. and Mohamad Amirul, A. A. (2019) The Influence of Social Commerce Factors on Customer Intention to Purchase, Asian Themes in Social Sciences Research, 3 (1), pp. 1-10.
[Online]. Available from: https://tinyurl.com/2f8res3e
[Accessed 3 November 2019].

Abu-Shamaa, R., Abu-Shanab, E. and Khasawneh, R. (2016) Payment Methods and Purchase Intention from Online Stores: An Empirical Study in Jordan, International Journal of E-Business Research (IJEBR), 12 (2), pp. 31-44.
[Online]. Available from: https://tinyurl.com/3cbe96pa
[Accessed 7 October 2019].

Adiwijaya, M. (2015) The Effect of Vendor Trustworthiness toward Online Purchase Intention through Costumer Trust, International Research Journal of Business Studies, 7 (3), pp. 189-197.
[Online]. Available from: https://tinyurl.com/hp8ru4ue
[Accessed 20 October 2019].

Agudo-Peregrina, A. F., Acquila-Natale, E. and Hernandez-Garcia, A. (2015) Is age still valid for segmenting e-shoppers?, 2nd International Symposium on Partial Least Squares Path Modeling, Seville, pp. 1-12.
[Online]. Available from: https://tinyurl.com/3wfwrkut
[Accessed 22 October 2019].

Agyapong, H. A. (2018) Exploring the Influential Factors of Online Purchase Intention in Finland, International Business, University of Applied Sciences, pp. 1-51.
[Online]. Available from: https://tinyurl.com/ent8aana
[Accessed 20 October 2019].

References

Ahmed, M. (2017) Estimating The Impact Of Need Fulfilment On Human Motivation According To Maslow's Hierarchy Of Needs, University of Akron, Akron, pp. 1-48.
[Online]. Available from: https://tinyurl.com/46z4kyev
[Accessed 23 October 2019].

Aithal, P. S. and Kumar, P. M. S. (2016) Comparative Analysis of Theory X, Theory Y, Theory Z, and Theory A for Managing People and Performance, International Journal of Scientific Research and Modern Education (IJSRME), 1 (1), pp. 803-812.
[Online]. Available from: https://tinyurl.com/2y4e4ws9
[Accessed 23 October 2019].

Akter, S. and Wamba, S. F. (2016) Big data analytics in E-commerce: a systematic review and agenda for future research, Electronic Markets, May, 26, pp. 173-194.
[Online]. Available from: https://tinyurl.com/ybeenwj9
[Accessed 3 July 2019].

Anghelache, C., Manole, A. and Anghel, M. G. (2015) Analysis of final consumption and gross investment influence on GDP - multiple linear regression model, Theoretical and Applied Economics, Autumn, XXII, 3 (604), pp. 137-142.
[Online]. Available from: https://tinyurl.com/4pvedht4
[Accessed 2 November 2019].

Ariffin, S. K., Mohan, T. and Goh, Y.-N. (2018) Influence of consumers' perceived risk on consumers' online purchase intention, Journal of Research in Interactive Marketing, 12 (3), pp. 309-327.
[Online]. Available from: https://tinyurl.com/2vkyxv2m
[Accessed 19 October 2019].

Arshad, Y., Ibrahim, S. N. S. and Chook, X. C. (2016) Successful Implementation of Quotewin Software Tendering System: A Case Study of a Multinational Company, Journal of Theoretical and Applied Information Technology, November, 93 (2), pp. 421-432.
[Online]. Available from: https://tinyurl.com/yc3mxjwy
[Accessed 14 May 2020].

Arshad, Y., Chin, W. P., Yahaya, S. N., Nizam, N. Z., Masrom, N. R. and Ibrahim, S. N. S. (2018) Small and Medium Enterprises' Adoption for E-Commerce in Malaysia Tourism State, International Journal of Academic Research in Business and Social Sciences, 8 (10), pp. 1447-1457.
[Online]. Available from: https://tinyurl.com/24yn4anr
[Accessed 15 May 2020].

Arulkumar, S. and Kannaiah, D. (2015) Predicting Purchase Intention of Online Consumers using Discriminant Analysis Approach, European Journal of Business and Management, 7 (4), pp. 319–323.
[Online]. Available from: https://tinyurl.com/3xdx62ps
[Accessed 23 October 2019].

Azrin, A., Tarofder, A. K. and Azam, S. M. F. (2018) Neuroticism Indifference to Brand Familiarity and Social Influence Towards Purchase Intention in Social Networking Services (SNS) in Malaysia, Asian Journal of Marketing, 12 (1), pp. 1-11.
[Online]. Available from: https://tinyurl.com/yeyv5nev
[Accessed 2 November 2019].

Barcelona Field Studies Centre (2020) Standard Deviation.
[Online]. Available from: https://tinyurl.com/2yunpkv7
[Accessed 5 April 2020].

References

Bavanandan, S., Ahmad, G., Teo, A.-H., Chen, L. and Liu, F. X. (2016) Budget Impact Analysis of Peritoneal Dialysis versus Conventional In-Center Hemodialysis in Malaysia, Value in Health Regional Issues, May, 9, pp. 8-14.
[Online]. Available from: https://tinyurl.com/2hxvzmbn
[Accessed 29 September 2019].

Bayer, E., Fachruddin and Torong, Z. B. (2018) The Influence Of Budget Goal Clarity, Internal Control System, Reporting System, With Organizational Commitment As Moderating Variable On The Performance Accountability Of Government Agencies Of Local Government Serdang Bedagai Regency, International Journal of Public Budgeting, Accounting and Finance, 1 (2), pp. 1-10.
[Online]. Available from: https://tinyurl.com/3pcarbsb
[Accessed 31 October 2019].

Beranek, L., Remes, R. and Nydl, V. (2017) Application of Structural Equation Modeling to Explain Online Shoppers' Response to Price Comparison Sites, ICEEG '17: Proceedings of the 1st International Conference on E-commerce, E-Business and E-Government, Turku, June, pp. 72-75.
[Online]. Available from: https://tinyurl.com/y378wnpa
[Accessed 7 October 2019].

Bhukya, R. and Singh, S. (2015) The effect of perceived risk dimensions on purchase intention: An empirical evidence from Indian private labels market, American Journal of Business, 30 (4), pp. 218-230.
[Online]. Available from: https://tinyurl.com/3ybfvd8z
[Accessed 20 October 2019].

Blanca, M. J., Alarcon, R., Arnau, J., Bono, R. and Bendayan, R. (2017) Non-normal data: Is ANOVA still a valid option?, Psicothema, 29 (4), pp. 552-557.
[Online]. Available from: https://tinyurl.com/yc4cc4jv
[Accessed 5 April 2020].

BMJ Publishing Group Ltd (2020) 11. Correlation and regression.
[Online]. Available from: https://tinyurl.com/yc5dw43b
[Accessed 5 April 2020].

Bulut, Z. A. (2015) Determinants of repurchase intention in online shopping: A Turkish consumer's perspective, International Journal of Business and Social Science, 6 (10), October, pp. 55-63.
[Online]. Available from: https://tinyurl.com/mr2296ss
[Accessed 19 October 2019].

Cain, M. K., Zhang, Z. and Yuan, K.-H. (2017) Univariate and multivariate skewness and kurtosis for measuring nonnormality: Prevalence, influence and estimation, Behav Res, 49, pp. 1716-1735.
[Online]. Available from: https://tinyurl.com/yx925u4e
[Accessed 26 March 2020].

Chakraborty, R., Lee, J., Bagchi-Sen, S., Upadhyaya, S. and Rao, H. R. (2016) Online shopping intention in the context of data breach in online retail stores: An examination of older and younger adults, Decision Support Systems, March, 83, pp. 47-56.
[Online]. Available from: https://tinyurl.com/nh9y35tm
[Accessed 20 October 2019].

Chang, W. and Chao, R.-F. (2018) The Impact of Shopping Values on Intention of Online Travel purchase for Mature Consumers: a Mediated Moderation Model, Journal of Tourism and Hospitality Management, June, 6 (1), pp. 92-99.
[Online]. Available from: https://tinyurl.com/bdzxhxn5
[Accessed 5 October 2019].

Chen, Y., Yan, X. and Fan, W. (2015) Examining the Effects of Decomposed Perceived Risk on Consumer Online Shopping Behavior: A field study in China, Engineering Economics, June, 26 (3), pp. 315-326.
[Online]. Available from: https://tinyurl.com/5ev2bxv7
[Accessed 20 October 2019].

References

Creswell, J. W. (2014) Research Design. 4th Edition. Thousand Oaks: Sage Publications, pp. 4-181.

Cronk, B. C. (2018) How to Use SPSS®: A Step-By-Step Guide to Analysis and Interpretation. 10th Edition. New York: Routledge.
[Online]. Available from: Google Books. https://tinyurl.com/3xvh356j
[Accessed 28 September 2019].

Dileep, K. M., Harvi, S. and Govindarajo, N. S. (2015) Malaysian Consumer Research: Does Computer Literacy Affirmative towards E-commerce Activities?, Journal of Economics and Behavioral Studies, February, 7 (1), pp. 50-63.
[Online]. Available from: https://tinyurl.com/3k42f9jv
[Accessed 27 July 2019].

Disatnik, D. and Sivan, L. (2016) The multicollinearity illusion in moderated regression analysis, Marketing Letters, June, 27, pp. 403-408.
[Online]. Available from: https://tinyurl.com/yc3acb4p
[Accessed 3 November 2019].

Duffett, R. G. (2017) Influence of social media marketing communications on young consumers' attitudes, Young Consumers, 18 (1), pp. 19-39.
[Online]. Available from: https://tinyurl.com/ydh2zrzr
[Accessed 12 October 2019].

Ekpe, I., Adubasim, E. I. and Adim, V. C. (2016) Effect Of Price, Advertising And Motivation On Online Purchase Behaviours Among Youth Academic Entrepreneurs In Nigeria: Social Influence As Moderator, International Journal of Entrepreneurship, 20 (1), pp. 42-56.
[Online]. Available from: https://tinyurl.com/5857jskv
[Accessed 24 October 2019].

Eldenburg, L. G., Brooks, A., Oliver, J., Vesty, G., Dormer, R., Murthy, V. and Pawsey, N. (2020) Management Accounting, 4th Edition, Milton Qtd 4064: John Wiley & Sons Australia Ltd, pp. 35-41.
[Online]. Available from: Google Books. https://tinyurl.com/2hwv57wf
[Accessed 8 May 2020].

Elliott, A. C. and Woodward, W. A. (2016) IBM SPSS by Example: A Practical Guide to Statistical Data Analysis, 2nd Edition, Thousand Oaks: Sage Publications Inc..
[Online]. Available from: Google Books. https://tinyurl.com/aupjy9x7
[Accessed 31 October 2019].

Escobar-Rodríguez, T. and Bonsón-Fernández, R. (2017) Analysing online purchase intention in Spain: fashion e-commerce, Information Systems and e-Business Management, August, 15, pp. 599-622.
[Online]. Available from: https://tinyurl.com/5n88yudu
[Accessed 1 October 2019].

Etikan, I., Musa, S. A. and Alkassim, R. S. (2016) Comparison of Convenience Sampling and Purposive Sampling, American Journal of Theoretical and Applied Statistics, 5 (1), pp. 1-4,
[Online]. Available from: https://tinyurl.com/bdhndhut
[Accessed 8 October 2019].

Fang, J., Wen, C., George, B. and Prybutok, V. R. (2016) Consumer Heterogeneity, Perceived Value, And Repurchase Decision-Making In Online Shopping: The Role Of Gender, Age, And Shopping Motives, Journal of Electronic Commerce Research, 17 (2), pp. 116-131.
[Online]. Available from: https://tinyurl.com/mrhabamf
[Accessed 3 October 2019].

Faryabi, M., Fesaghandis, K. S. and Saed, M. (2015) Brand Name, Sales Promotion and Consumers' Online Purchase Intention for Cell-phone Brands, International Journal of Marketing Studies, 7 (1), pp. 167-179.
[Online]. Available from: https://tinyurl.com/5f39u5pe
[Accessed 24 October 2019].

References

Fatin, Z. A. W., Noor, F. M. and Kalsitinoor, S. (2019) Investigating The Factors Of Trust And Risk On Career Women In Luxury Brand Purchasing Intention Through Online In Malaysia, International Journal of Accounting, Finance and Business, June, 4 (19), pp. 108-122.
[Online]. Available from: https://tinyurl.com/y69rxswf
[Accessed 17 November 2019].

Finch, W. H., Bolin, J. E. and Kelley, K. (2019) Multilevel Modeling Using R, 2nd Edition, New York, CRC Press, pp. 1-19.
[Online]. Available from: Google Books. https://tinyurl.com/yc6hfhar
[Accessed 7 April 2020].

Ghandour, A. (2015) Ecommerce Website Value Model For Smes, International Journal of Electronic Commerce Studies, 6 (2), pp. 203-222.
[Online]. Available from: https://tinyurl.com/3fjvfs33
[Accessed 5 June 2019].

Ghouri, M. A., ul Haq, M. A. and Khan, N. R. (2017) Customer Perception on Online Purchase Intention: The Impact of Online Shopping Orientations On Online Buying Intention, The Eurasia Proceedings of Science, Technology, Engineering & Mathematics (EPSTEM), 1, pp. 76-82.
[Online]. Available from: https://tinyurl.com/3ehw456b
[Accessed 2 November 2019].

GoodData Documentation (2020) Normality Testing - Skewness and Kurtosis.
[Online]. Available from: https://tinyurl.com/mry4r3cv
[Accessed 4 April 2020].

Grundmann, N., Yohannes, Y., Silverberg, M., Balakrishnan, J. M., Krishnan, S. V. and Arquilla, B. (2017) Workplace violence in the emergency department in India and the United States, International Journal of Academic Medicine, 3 (2), pp. 248-255.
[Online]. Available from: https://tinyurl.com/4xc98kua
[Accessed 15 April 2020].

Hajli, N., Sims, J., Zadeh, A. H. and Richard, M.-O. (2017) A social commerce investigation of the role of trust in a social networking site on purchase intentions, Journal of Business Research, February, 71, pp. 133-141.
[Online]. Available from: https://tinyurl.com/yu2b3tew
[Accessed 20 October 2019].

Hart, P. D. (2018) Multivariate multiple regression analysis of fitness and sociodemographic variables in adults, International Journal of Physical Education, Sports and Health, August, 5 (5), pp. 84-86.
[Online]. Available from: https://tinyurl.com/557yp6sw
[Accessed 6 April 2020].

Hashmi, H., Attiq, S. and Rasheed, F. (2019) Factors Affecting Online Impulsive Buying Behavior: A Stimulus Organism Response Model Approach, Market Forces College of Management Sciences, June, 14 (1), pp. 19-42.
[Online]. Available from: https://tinyurl.com/2p9hd276
[Accessed 19 November 2019].

Hattangadi, V. (2015) Theory X & Theory Y, International Journal of Recent Research Aspects, December, 2 (4), pp. 20-21.
[Online]. Available from: https://tinyurl.com/2w8472p6
[Accessed 23 October 2019].

Hazra, A. and Gogtay, N. (2016) Biostatistics Series Module 6: Correlation and Linear Regression, Indian Journal of Dermatology, November-December, 61 (6), pp. 593-601.
[Online]. Available from: https://tinyurl.com/2awp4db2
[Accessed 15 April 2020].

Hinton, P. R. and McMurray, I. (2017) Presenting Your Data with SPSS Explained, 1st Edition, New York: Routledge, pp. 145-155.
[Online]. Available from: Google Books. https://tinyurl.com/yurzjbyz
[Accessed 9 April 2020].

References

Hong, I. B. (2015) Understanding the consumer's online merchant selection process: The roles of product involvement, perceived risk, and trust expectation, International Journal of Information Management, June, 35 (3), pp. 322-336.
[Online]. Available from: https://tinyurl.com/3tmjhy5j
[Accessed 19 October 2019].

Insua, M., Frias, Z. and Perez Martinez, J. (2017) Application of multiple regression analysis to the prices of the spectrum in the IMT band, 28th European Regional Conference of the International Telecommunications Society (ITS): "Competition and Regulation in the Information Age", Passau, 30 July - 2 August, Calgary: International Telecommunications Society, pp. 1-12.
[Online]. Available from: https://tinyurl.com/2ysdvd8r
[Accessed 6 April 2020].

Irianto, H. (2015) Consumers' Attitude and Intention Towards Organic Food Purchase: An Extension of Theory of Planned Behavior in Gender Perspective, International Journal of Management, Economics and Social Sciences, March, 4 (1), pp. 17-31.
[Online]. Available from: https://tinyurl.com/6fx34nth
[Accessed 5 October 2019].

Islam, M. R. (2018) Sample Size and Its Role in Central Limit Theorem (CLT), Computational and Applied Mathematics Journal, February, 4 (1) pp. 1-7.
[Online]. Available from: https://tinyurl.com/mps5bpba
[Accessed 6 October 2019].

Jadhav, V. and Khanna, M. (2016) Factors Influencing Online Buying Behavior of College Students: A Qualitative Analysis, The Qualitative Report, 21 (1), 1, pp. 1-15.
[Online]. Available from: https://tinyurl.com/46chuse2
[Accessed 5 October 2019].

Jamil, B. and Mimi, L. A. (2016) Intention to use Social Media Tools Among Business-To-Consumer (B2C) Practitioners in Klang Valley, Malaysia: Insight from TPB, Malaysian Management Review, July –December, 51 (2), pp. 57-66.
[Online]. Available from: htttps://tinyurl.com/bddhc3ba
[Accessed 1 October 2019].

Jeon, J. (2015) The Strengths and Limitations of the Statistical Modeling of Complex Social Phenomenon: Focusing on SEM, Path Analysis, or Multiple Regression Models, International Journal of Social, Behavioral, Educational, Economic, Business and Industrial Engineering, 9 (5), pp. 1634-1642.
[Online]. Available from: https://tinyurl.com/335ta734
[Accessed 3 November 2019].

Joshi, A., Kale, S., Chandel, S. and Pal, D. K. (2015) Likert Scale: Explored and Explained, British Journal of Applied Science & Technology, February, 7 (4), pp. 396-403.
[Online]. Available from: https://tinyurl.com/mr3kffx2
[Accessed 28 September 2019].

Kamboj, S. and Rahman, Z. (2016) The influence of user participation in social media-based brand communities on brand loyalty: age and gender as moderators, Journal of Brand Management, November, 23 (6), pp. 679-700.
[Online]. Available from: https://tinyurl.com/39m63umh
[Accessed 19 October 2019].

Kanchan, U., Kumar, N. and Gupta, A. (2015) A Study Of Online Purchase Behaviour Of Customers In India, Ictact Journal on Management Studies, August, 1 (3), pp. 136-142.
[Online]. Available from: https://tinyurl.com/bdud8539
[Accessed 12 October 2019].

References

Kartiwi, M., Hussin, H., Suhaimi, M. A., Jalaldeen, M. R. M. and Amin, M. R. (2018) Impact of external factors on determining E-commerce benefits among SMEs in Malaysia, Journal of Global Entrepreneurship Research, July, 8 (18), pp. 1-12.
[Online]. Available from: https://tinyurl.com/mufvkhtf
[Accessed 19 September 2019].

Kasim, M., Muhammad Nasri, M. H. and Nor Pujawati, M. S. (2018) The Moderating Effect Of Islamic Practices On The Relationship Between Online Security And Customers' Loyalty In Online Purchasing In Malaysia, Journal of Global Business and Social Entrepreneurship, December, 4 (13), pp. 82-95.
[Online]. Available from: https://tinyurl.com/4wbetz64
[Accessed 24 May 2020].

Kaur, J., Wadera, D., and Sethi, R. S. (2018) Purchase Intention Survey of Millennials Towards Online Fashion Stores, Academy of Marketing Studies Journal, 22 (1).
[Online]. Available from: https://tinyurl.com/55h9r27b
[Accessed 2 October 2019].

Khan, A., Rehman, H. and Rehman, S.-u.- (2013) An Empirical Analysis of Correlation Between Technostress and Job Satisfaction: A Case of KPK, Pakistan, Pakistan Journal Of Library and Information Science, 14 (2013), pp. 9-15.
[Online]. Available from: https://tinyurl.com/yemer4rj
[Accessed 8 May 2020].

Khan, S. A., Liang, Y. and Shahzad, S. (2015) An empirical study of perceived factors affecting customer satisfaction to re-purchase intention in online stores in China, Journal of Service Science and Management, June, 8, pp. 291-305.
[Online]. Available from: https://tinyurl.com/27f9fhb3
[Accessed 12 October 2019].

Khan, A. G. (2016) Electronic Commerce: A Study on Benefits and Challenges in an Emerging Economy, Global Journal of Management and Business Research: B Economics and Commerce, 16 (1).
[Online]. Available from: https://tinyurl.com/5xex3uwu
[Accessed 1 June 2019].

Kharel, B. (2018) Factors Influencing Online Brand Trust: Evidence from Online Buyers in Kathmandu Valley, Journal of Business and Social Sciences Research, 3 (1), pp. 47-64.
[Online]. Available from: https://tinyurl.com/ywxcn55v
 [Accessed 5 October 2019].

Kim, J. H. (2019) Multicollinearity and misleading statistical results, Korean Journal of Anesthesiology, December, 72 (6), pp. 558-569.
[Online]. Available from: https://tinyurl.com/ynxabm65
[Accessed 9 April 2020].

Kim, G. and Koo, H. (2016) The causal relationship between risk and trust in the online marketplace: A bidirectional perspective, Computers in Human Behavior, February, 55 (B), pp. 1020-1029.
[Online]. Available from: https://tinyurl.com/3eesy2ub
[Accessed 19 October 2019].

Knight, G. P. (2018) A Survey of Some Important Techniques and Issues in Multiple Regression. In: Kieras, D. E. and Just, M. A., New Methods in Reading Comprehension Research, London: Taylor and Francis Group, pp. 11-28.
[Online]. Available from: Taylor and Francis Group. https://tinyurl.com/3mf332da
[Accessed 2 November 2019].

References

Kowang, T. O., Jacob, R. A., Yew, L. K., Hee, O. C., Fei, G. C. and Long, C. S. (2019) E-commerce Advertising: Does the Traditional Advertising Elements Still Relevant? International Journal of Academic Research in Business & Social Sciences, 9 (7), pp. 191-201.
[Online]. Available from: https://tinyurl.com/mvdm3udr
[Accessed 29 May 2020].

Laerd Statistics (2018) Moderator Analysis with a Dichotomous Moderator using SPSS Statistics.
[Online]. Available from: https://tinyurl.com/2s3kpzev
[Accessed 31 October 2019].

Laub, J. A. (2019) Random Sample.
[Online]. Available from: https://tinyurl.com/4bbfsy36
[Accessed 6 October 2019].

Li, Z. and Hou, A. C. Y. (2019) Online Purchases Preference And Personal Characteristics: A Moderation Approach, International Journal of Electronic Commerce Studies, 10 (1), pp. 1-21.
[Online]. Available from: https://tinyurl.com/3634bnu7
[Accessed 22 October 2019].

Liebana-Cabanillas, F. and Alonso-Dos-Santos, M. (2017) Factors that determine the adoption of Facebook commerce: The moderating effect of age, Journal of Engineering and Technology Management, April, 44, pp. 1-18.
[Online]. Available from: https://tinyurl.com/226n3wfc
[Accessed 19 October 2019].

Liew, Y. S. and Falahat, M. (2019) Factors influencing consumers' purchase intention towards online group buying in Malaysia, International Journal of Electronic Marketing and Retailing, 10 (1), pp. 60-77.
[Online]. Available from: https://tinyurl.com/ya78vndu
[Accessed 17 May 2019].

Lim, S. C., Baharudin, A. S. and Low, R. Q. (2016) E-Commerce Adoption In Peninsula Malaysia: Perceived Strategic Value As Moderator In The Relationship Between Perceived Barriers, Organizational Readiness And Competitor Pressure, Journal of Theoretical and Applied Information Technology, September, 91 (2), pp. 228-237.
[Online]. Available from: https://tinyurl.com/yc75f8m4
[Accessed 27 September 2019].

Lim, Y. J., Abdullah, O., Abd., R. R. and Yusuf, H.-O. (2015) Attitude towards Online Shopping Activities in Malaysia Public University, Mediterranean Journal of Social Sciences, March, 6 (2), pp. 456-462.
[Online]. Available from: https://tinyurl.com/2p4mwxpe
[Accessed 5 June 2019].

Lim, Y. J., Abdullah, O., Shahrul, S. N., Abdul, R. R. and Safizal, A. (2016) Factors Influencing Online Shopping Behavior: The Mediating Role of Purchase Intention, Procedia Economics and Finance, 35 (2016), pp. 401-410.
[Online]. Available from: https://tinyurl.com/avzp4u6s
[Accessed 1 October 2019].

Lim, Y. S., Azizah, O. and Ramayah, T. (2015) Online Purchase: A Study of Generation Y in Malaysia, International Journal of Business and Management, May, 10 (6), pp. 1-7.
[Online]. Available from: https://tinyurl.com/mr3hvwym
[Accessed 1 August 2019].

Liu, Y. and Wu, Y. (2019) On the Influencing Factors of Consumer's Purchasing Behavior in Online Group Buying—— Taking Group Buying of Catering as an Example, 1st International Conference on Business, Economics, Management Science, Advances in Economics, Business and Management Research, 80, pp. 552-557.
[Online]. Available from: https://tinyurl.com/t6ben4re
[Accessed 9 October 2019].

References

Mahamid, I. (2019) The Development of Regression Models for Preliminary Prediction of Road Construction Duration, International Journal of Engineering and Information Systems, April, 3 (4), pp. 14-20.
[Online]. Available from: https://tinyurl.com/4e8ud8hf
[Accessed 21 May 2020].

Maia, C., Lunardi, G., Longaray, A. and Munhoz, P. (2018) Factors and characteristics that influence consumers' participation in social commerce, Revista de Gestão, 25 (2), pp. 194-211.
[Online]. Available from: https://tinyurl.com/3vm2yxby
[Accessed 23 October 2019].

Majid, M. and Firend, Al. R. (2017) Social Media, Online Shopping Activities and Perceived Risks in Malaysia, International Journal of Economics And Financial Management, 1 (1), pp. 12-24.
[Online]. Available from: https://tinyurl.com/mvpff62t
[Accessed 5 October 2019].

Mazzini, M., Rohani, M. and Salwana, H. (2016) Online Purchase Behavior of Generation Y in Malaysia, Procedia Economics and Finance, 37, pp. 292-298.
[Online]. Available from: https://tinyurl.com/muw3w6mu
[Accessed 19 October 2019].

Meera, V. and Gayathri, R. (2018) Millennial Consumer Satisfaction on Online Shopping In Pollachi Taluk, SELP Journal of Social Science, July-September, ix (38), pp. 15-20.
[Online]. Available from: https://tinyurl.com/2z8pe8bv
[Accessed 20 October 2019].

Mkubukeli, Z. and Cronje, J. C. (2018) Pull and Push Elements of Entrepreneurship in South Africa: A Small-scale Mining Perspective, Journal of Entrepreneurship & Organization Management, 7 (3), pp. 1-7.
[Online]. Available from: https://tinyurl.com/2emjysne
[Accessed 1 August 2019].

Mohd Fawzy, A. B., Sharuddin, S. H., Rajagderan, S. and Wan Zulkifly, W. Z. (2018) E-Commerce Adoption And An Analysis Of The Popular E-Commerce Business Sites In Malaysia, Journal of Internet Banking and Commerce.
[Online]. Available from: https://tinyurl.com/yt9j9cat
[Accessed 5 June 2019].

Morey, R. D., Hoekstra, R., Rouder, J. N., Lee, M. D., Wagenmakers, E. -J. (2016) The fallacy of placing confidence in confidence intervals, Psychonomic Bulletin & Review, February, 23, pp. 103-123.
[Online]. Available from: https://tinyurl.com/2eb4hnj2
[Accessed 27 September 2019].

Moslehpour, M., Tumurbaatar, J., Amri, K. and Batmunkh, M.-U. (2016) What Do Mongolian Facebook Users Want from Advertisers? International Journal of Business and Management, August, 11 (9), pp. 51-62.
[Online]. Available from: https://tinyurl.com/3zdhpz5a
[Accessed 31 October 2019].

Mostafa, R. H. A. and Elsedi, R. I. (2018) Factors affecting consumers' willingness to buy private label brands (PLBs) Applied study on hypermarkets, Spanish Journal of Marketing, 22 (3), pp. 341-361.
[Online]. Available from: https://tinyurl.com/2h65yrf2
[Accessed 3 November 2019].

Muhammad Dharma, T. P. N., Rossanty, Y., Ku Halim, K. A. and Nurliyana Izzati, M. Z. (2019) An empirical examination of the factors influencing consumer's purchase intention toward online shopping, Journal of Business and Retail Management Research, July, 13 (4), pp. 14-29.
[Online]. Available from: https://tinyurl.com/357pvftr
[Accessed 19 November 2019].

References

Myers, M. D. (2020) Qualitative Research in Business and Management, 3rd Edition, Sage Publications Ltd: London, pp. 1-10.
[Online]. Available from: Google Books. https://tinyurl.com/n6zehk9f
[Accessed 10 October 2019].

Namdeo, S. K. and Rout, S. D. (2016) Calculating and interpreting Cronbach's alpha using Rosenberg assessment scale on paediatrician's attitude and perception on self esteem, International Journal of Community Medicine and Public Health, June, 3 (6), pp. 1371-1374.
[Online]. Available from: https://tinyurl.com/y89k93zv
[Accessed 7 May 2020].

Ndie, E. C., Anene, J. O. and Ezenduka, P. O. (2019) Assessment of Effect of Peer Pressure and Mass Media on Secondary School Students Involvement in Premarital Sex in Anambra State of Nigeria, Journal of Health Science, 7, pp. 227-232.
[Online]. Available from: https://tinyurl.com/497pawkv
[Accessed 31 July 2019].

Ng, C. W., Chong, Y. W. and Mohmad, Y. S. (2017) Effect of Leadership Styles, Social Capital, and Social Entrepreneurship on Organizational Effectiveness of Social Welfare Organization in Malaysia: Data Screening and Preliminary Analysis, International Review of Management and Marketing, 7 (2), pp. 117-122.
[Online]. Available from: https://tinyurl.com/4ez5akzw
[Accessed 25 November 2019].

Nor Hazlin, N. A., Nurazariah, A. and Hafizzah, B. B. (2016) Perceived Quality and Emotional Value that Influence Consumer's Purchase Intention towards American and Local Products, Procedia Economics and Finance, 35, pp. 639-643.
[Online]. Available from: https://tinyurl.com/5as9392r
[Accessed 27 November 2019].

Noorshella, C. N., Abdullah, A. M., Nurul Hasliana, H. and Mohd Nazri, M. (2019) Effect of Consumer Demographics and Risk Factors on Online Purchase Behaviour in Malaysia, MDPI, 9 (1), 10, pp. 1-11.
[Online]. Available from: https://tinyurl.com/wtsx2sm6
[Accessed 18 November 2019].

Nurlaily, I., Noermijati and Hussein, A. S. (2017) Influence of Life Style and Attitude Toward Trust and Repeat Purchase Intentions on Social Media Users (Study On Instagram Users in Malang), Wacana, 20 (2), (2017), pp. 68-78.
[Online]. Available from: https://tinyurl.com/ejy2rmd3
[Accessed 7 October 2019].

Nurul, A. H., Abdullah, O., Safizal, A., Shahrul, N. S., Nor Faizzah, R. and Hazalina, M. S. (2016) The Relationship of Attitude, Subjective Norm and Website Usability on Consumer Intention to Purchase Online: An Evidence of Malaysian Youth, Procedia Economics and Finance, 35, pp. 493-502.
[Online]. Available from: https://tinyurl.com/2bu3wfv7
[Accessed 27 November 2019].

Ocloo, C. E., Hu, X., Akaba, S., Addai, M., Worwui-Brown, D. and Spio-Kwofie, A. (2018) B2B E-Commerce Adoption amongst Manufacturing SMEs: Evidence from Ghana, Australian Journal of Economics And Management Science, January-December, 8 (1), pp. 126-146.
[Online]. Available from: https://tinyurl.com/adr69e6c
[Accessed 5 June 2019].

Okagbue, H. I., Adamu, M. O., Edeki, S. O. and Opanuga, A. A. (2016) On the Use of Some Selected Estimators in the Computation of Interactions in a Moderated Multiple Regression of a Masked Survey Data, International Business Management, 10 (4), pp. 352-356.
[Online]. Available from: https://tinyurl.com/3cjh9utd
[Accessed 5 April 2020].

References

Oladapo, V. and Onyeaso, G. (2018) Empirical Investigation of the Moderating Effects of Organizational Size on Ecommerce Capabilities and Organizational Performance, International Journal of Economics, Business and Finance, August, 5 (1), pp. 1-9.
[Online]. Available from: https://tinyurl.com/mrycwn65
[Accessed 4 June 2019].

Oliveria, T., Alhinho, M., Rita, P. and Dhillon, G. (2017) Modelling and testing consumer trust dimensions in e-commerce, Computers in Human Behavior, June, 71, pp. 153-164.
[Online]. Available from: https://tinyurl.com/3sxdu5pc
[Accessed 20 October 2019].

O' Reilly Media Inc. (2020) A.4 F-Distribution.
[Online]. Available from: https://tinyurl.com/49mbf7be
[Accessed 5 April 2020].

Othman, S. and Shahzad, A. (2016) The Mediating Effects Of Behavioural Intention Of The Acceptance And Use Of E-Commerce Among SMEs In Kedah, Malaysia, Sci. Int. (Lahore), May-June, 28 (3), pp. 3173-3178.
[Online]. Available from: https://tinyurl.com/mr2kx248
[Accessed 13 July 2019].

Pauzi, S. F. F., Thoo, A. C., Tan, L. C., Muharam, F. M. and Talib, N. A. (2017) Factors Influencing Consumers Intention for Online Grocery Shopping – A Proposed Framework, IOP Conference Series: Materials Science and Engineering, 215 (2017), pp. 1-12.
[Online]. Available from: https://tinyurl.com/3kn6zeux
[Accessed 5 October 2019].

Penzol, M. J., de Pablo, G. S., Llorente, C., Moreno, C., Hernandez, P., Dorado, M. L. and Parellada, M. (2019) Functional Gastrointestinal Disease in Autism Spectrum Disorder: A Retrospective Descriptive Study in a Clinical Sample, Frontiers in Psychiatry, April, 10 (179), pp. 1-6.
[Online]. Available from: https://tinyurl.com/239kja4n
[Accessed 25 November 2019].

Phang, S. F., Lee, Z. W. and Nabilah, B. M. Y. (2019) Gender Differences In Impulsivity Of E-Commerce Online Purchase Intention Among UTAR Students: Conscientiousness, Negative Emotionality And Extraversion As Covariates, Universiti Tunku Abdul Rahman, Faculty of Art and Social Science, August, pp. 1-100.
[Online]. Available from: https://tinyurl.com/3bsb6m3c
[Accessed 1 October 2019].

Rahman, M. S. (2017) The Advantages and Disadvantages of Using Qualitative and Quantitative Approaches and Methods in Language "Testing and Assessment" Research: A Literature Review, Journal of Education and Learning, 6 (1), pp. 102-112.
[Online]. Available from: https://tinyurl.com/4whcbftj
[Accessed 1 October 2019].

Rezaei, S., Emami, M. and Valaei, N. (2016) The Moderating Impact of Product Classification on the Relationship between Online Trust, Satisfaction, and Repurchase Intention. Encyclopedia of E-Commerce Development, Implementation, and Management, pp. 1674-1692.
[Online]. Available from: https://tinyurl.com/4dkpekj9
[Accessed 19 October 2019].

Rrumbullaku, J. and Kume, K. (2017) The advantages of online shopping according to Albanian customers, THESIS, 6 (3), pp. 77-91.
[Online]. Available from: https://tinyurl.com/5avya95v
[Accessed 7 October 2019].

References

Said, J. and Maryono, M. (2018) Motivation and Perception of Tourists as Push and Pull Factors to Visit National Park, E3S Web of Conferences, 31 (08022), pp. 1-5.
[Online]. Available from: https://tinyurl.com/ywyxuy8k
[Accessed 1 October 2019].

Saif-Ur-Rehman and Rizwan, A. (2016) A Study of Barriers to E-Commerce Adoption among SMEs in Malaysia, College of Business, University of Modern Sciences, Dubai, UAE, 1 (1), pp. 45-58.
[Online]. Available from: https://tinyurl.com/yncr44xy
[Accessed 1 June 2019].

Sharifi Fard, S., Tamam, E., Hj Hassan, M. S., Waheed, M. and Zaremohzzabieh, Z. (2016) Factors affecting Malaysian university students' purchase intention in social networking sites, Cogent Business & Management, 3 (1), pp. 1-12.
[Online]. Available from: https://tinyurl.com/4tur2ba4
[Accessed 22 October 2019].

Sanwal, T., Avasthi, S. and Saxena, S. (2016) E-Commerce and its sway on the minds of young Generation, International Journal of Scientific and Research Publications, March, 6 (3), pp. 112-117.
[Online]. Available from: https://tinyurl.com/mz6zp3me
[Accessed 1 June 2019].

Schurink, E. (2019) The role of perceived social presence in online shopping The effects of chatbot appearance on perceived social presence, satisfaction and purchase intention, University of Twente, pp. 1-59.
[Online]. Available from: https://tinyurl.com/5y4kbr8t
[Accessed 22 October 2019].

Selvaraju, K. and Karthikeyan, P. (2016) Impact on E-Commerce towards Online Shopping and Customer Buying Behavior, Asian Journal of Research in Social Sciences and Humanities, July, 6 (7), pp. 1260-1270.
[Online]. Available from: https://tinyurl.com/5n93r2rp
[Accessed 20 October 2019].

Sethna, B. N., Hazari, S. and Bergiel, B. (2017) Influence of user generated content in online shopping: impact of gender on purchase behaviour, trust, and intention to purchase, Int. J. Electronic Marketing and Retailing, 8 (4), pp. 344-371.
[Online]. Available from: htttps://tinyurl.com/97kes8vt
[Accessed 12 October 2019].

Shafi, M. A., Rusiman, M. S., Hamzah, N. S. A., Nor, M. E., Ahmad, N., Azmi, N. A. H. M., Latip, M. F. A. and Azman, A. H. (2018) The analysis of morphometric data on rocky mountain wolves and artic wolves using statistical method, IOP Conf. Series: Journal of Physics: Conference Series, 995 (2018), pp. 1-10.
[Online]. Available from: https://tinyurl.com/9vvjtd99
[Accessed 5 April 2020].

Shanthi, R. and Kannaiah, D. (2015) Consumers' Perception on Online Shopping, Journal of Marketing and Consumer Research, 13, pp. 14-20.
[Online]. Available from: https://tinyurl.com/499c4z2p
[Accessed 6 October 2019].

Shaouf, A., Lu, K. and Li, X. (2016) The effect of web advertising visual design on online purchase intention: An examination across gender, Computers in Human Behavior, July, 60, pp. 622-634.
[Online]. Available from: https://tinyurl.com/5f646yr8
[Accessed 24 October 2019].

References

Sharma, N. (2017) A Study On Consumer Perceived Risk Towards Online Shopping In Certain Cities Of Gujarat, Gujarat Technological University, Ahmedabad, December, pp. 1-157.
[Online]. Available from: https://tinyurl.com/4pasmenb
[Accessed 11 October 2019].

Shekhar, P., Prince, M., Finelli, C., Demonbrun, M. and Waters, C. (2019) Integrating quantitative and qualitative research methods to examine student resistance to active learning, European Journal of Engineering Education, 44 (1-2), pp. 6-18.
[Online]. Available from: https://tinyurl.com/yxnxf73j
[Accessed 1 October 2019].

Silva, J., Pinho, J. C., Soares, A. and Sa, E. (2019) Antecedents Of Online Purchase Intention And Behaviour: Uncovering Unobserved Heterogeneity, Journal of Business Economics and Management, 20 (1), pp. 131-148.
[Online]. Available from: https://tinyurl.com/5azr37m6
[Accessed 22 October 2019].

Soikliew, K. and Araveeporn, A. (2018) Modifications of Levene's and O'Brien's Tests for Testing the Homogeneity of Variance Based on Median and Trimmed Mean, Thailand Statistician, July, 16 (2), pp. 106-128.
[Online]. Available from: https://tinyurl.com/bdd92rx8
[Accessed 3 April 2020].

Sook, H. P., Nur, A. T., Kiew, B. P. and Wei, Y. K. (2017) Evaluation of Self Management Behavior of Chronic Kidney Disease Patients, Journal of Pharmacy and Pharmacology, 5, pp. 179-188.
[Online]. Available from: https://tinyurl.com/wvfed3s3
[Accessed 29 March 2020].

Statistics Solutions (2020) Regression.
[Online]. Available from: https://tinyurl.com/2dbyb8sh
[Accessed 8 May 2020].

Stehlik-Barry, K. and Babinec, A. J. (2017) Data Analysis with IBM SPSS Statistics, 1st Edition, Birmingham: Packt Publishing Ltd., pp. 1-2.
[Online]. Available from: Google Books. https://tinyurl.com/2twpufnu
[Accessed 31 October 2019].

Suhan, J. (2015) Acceptance of Online Shopping in Bangladesh: Consumer's Perspective, IOSR Journal of Business and Management, January, 17 (1, II), pp. 14-24.
[Online]. Available from: https://tinyurl.com/yc3jbatu
[Accessed 11 October 2019].

Suryanegara, M., Andriyanto, F. and Winarko, B. (2017) What Changes after switching to 4G-LTE? Findings from the Indonesian Market, IEEE Access, 5, pp. 17070-17076.
[Online]. Available from: https://tinyurl.com/mu4nj7yj
[Accessed 20 October 2019].

Taber, K. S. (2018) The Use of Cronbach's Alpha When Developing and Reporting Research Instruments in Science Education, Research in Science Education, December, 48, pp. 1273-1296.
[Online]. Available from: https://tinyurl.com/ymdp2xaw
[Accessed 1 October 2019].

Tamar, S. H., Hooshiar, S. H., Karamimagham, S. and Poursadeghfard, M. (2016) Epidemiology and Descriptive Analysis of Neuro-Critical Care Unit; Shiraz, South of Iran, Archives of Anesthesiology & Critical Care, Summer, 2 (3), pp. 210-215.
[Online]. Available from: https://tinyurl.com/2styew76
[Accessed 18 November 2019].

Tan, K. W. (2018) Website Quality Social Activities and Online Purchase Intention in Malaysia, Master of Business Administration, Universiti Tunku Abdul Rahman, pp. 1-103.
[Online]. Available from: https://tinyurl.com/3m3hvxx6
[Accessed 18 November 2019].

References

Tanadi, T., Samadi, B. and Gharleghi, B. (2015) The Impact of Perceived Risks and Perceived Benefits to Improve an Online Intention among Generation-Y in Malaysia, Asian Social Science, September, 11 (26), pp. 226-238.
[Online]. Available from: https://tinyurl.com/mrxfuabv
[Accessed 3 October 2019].

The Star (2019) E-commerce transactions enjoying healthy growth.
[Online]. Available from: https://tinyurl.com/866aap5n
[Accessed 13 July 2019].

Thirumoorthi, T. and Wong, K. M. (2015) Tourism, In: Aida, I., S. Moghavvemi and Ghazali, M., Selected Theories In Social Science Research, Kuala Lumpur: University of Malaya Press, pp. 273-286.

Tseng, S.-M., Wu, J.-R., Chou, C.-W. and Tsai, H.-L. (2017) A study on Consumer Evaluations of Continued Group-Buying Intentions, International Journal of Innovative Science, Engineering & Technology, June, 4 (6), pp. 356-366.
[Online]. Available from: https://tinyurl.com/599jtw7v
[Accessed 9 October 2019].

UCLA (2020a) Regression Analysis | SPSS Annotated Output.
[Online]. Available from: https://tinyurl.com/563m7e3d
[Accessed 8 May 2020].

UCLA (2020b) Regression With SPSS Chapter 1 - Simple and Multiple Regression.
[Online]. Available from: https://tinyurl.com/4zkxhhez
[Accessed 8 May 2020].

Uysal, H. T., Aydemir, S. and Genc, E. (2017) Maslow's Hierarchy Of Needs In 21st Century: The Examination Of Vocational Differences, In: Researches on Science and Art in 21st Century Turkey, Arapgirlioğlu, H., Elliott, R. L., Turgeon, E. and Atik, A. (eds.), 1, Gece Kitaplığı, pp. 211-227.
[Online]. Available from: https://tinyurl.com/mv7wyarm
[Accessed 24 October 2019].

Vogler, S., Schneider, P. and Zimmermann, N. (2017) Price comparison of high-cost medicines 2017, Gesundheit Österreich, Vienna, August, pp. 1-43.
[Online]. Available from: https://tinyurl.com/39ym8dxm
[Accessed 7 October 2019].

Vyas, A. and Bissa, G. (2017) A Study on Customer Preference towards Online Shopping with Special Reference to Bikaner City, International Journal of Engineering Technology Science and Research, September, 4 (9), pp. 675-681.
[Online]. Available from: https://tinyurl.com/msscc3jf
[Accessed 11 October 2019].

Watts, M. (2016) Programmatic Advertising: Shaping Consumer Behavior or Invading Consumer Privacy?, Fisher College of Business, Ohio State University, pp. 1-28.
[Online]. Available from: https://tinyurl.com/3d5k2uxk
[Accessed 24 October 2019].

Weng, M. L. (2015) The Influence of Internet Advertising and Electronic Word of Mouth on Consumer Perceptions and Intention: Some Evidence from Online Group Buying, Journal of Computer Information Systems, 55 (4), pp. 81-89.
[Online]. Available from: https://tinyurl.com/wj3jy3mp
[Accessed 24 October 2019].

Worldometers (2020) Malaysia Population (LIVE).
[Online]. Available from: https://tinyurl.com/4cdy8r2r
[Accessed 3 May 2020].

Wu, S.-I. and Tsai, H.-T. (2017) A Comparison of the Online Shopping Behavior Patterns of Consumer Groups with Different Online Shopping Experiences, International Journal of Marketing Studies, May, 9 (3), pp. 24-38.
[Online]. Available from: https://tinyurl.com/3fce7hjs
[Accessed 7 October 2019].

References

Yockey, R. D. (2016) SPSS Demystified: A Step-by-Step Guide to Successful Data Analysis For SPSS Version 18.0, 2nd Edition, New York, Routledge, pp. 51-57.
[Online]. Available from: Google Books. https://tinyurl.com/nha7xem2
[Accessed 7 May 2020].

Zhao, X., Deng, S. and Zhou, Y. (2017) The impact of reference effects on online purchase intention of agricultural products: The moderating role of consumers' food safety consciousness, Internet Research, 27 (2), pp. 233-255.
[Online]. Available from: https://tinyurl.com/3awktk9t
[Accessed 19 October 2019].

Zhao, X. and Wan, H. L. (2017) Drivers of online purchase intention on Singles' Day: a study of Chinese consumers, International Journal of Electronic Marketing and Retailing, 8 (1).
[Online]. Available from: https://tinyurl.com/5af47tk7
[Accessed 2 November 2019].

Zhu, W. (2016) $p < 0.05$, < 0.01, < 0.001, < 0.0001, < 0.00001, < 0.000001, or < 0.0000001…, Journal of Sport and Health Science, March, 5 (1), pp. 77-79.
[Online]. Available from: https://tinyurl.com/52kbaz9b
[Accessed 4 April 2020].

Zoha, R., Kumaran, S., Hasmah, Z. and Mohd Hairul Nizam, M. N. (2017) SM Analytics: Impact of SM Engagement Metrics on Online Purchase Intention, Journal of Engineering and Applied Sciences, 12 (2), pp. 283-289.
[Online]. Available from: https://tinyurl.com/yuxmc5nd
[Accessed 27 November 2019].

Why Malaysian Consumers Prefer Online Purchases

APPENDIX A

Questionnaire for the Research Project

A survey on factors affecting online purchase intention among customers in Malaysia.

———

I'm running a research project to get more knowledge and understanding about the factors affecting the online purchase intention of people who shop online in Malaysia with e-commerce. Your participation in this project is desired.

The questionnaire shouldn't take more than 5 minutes to complete. The questionnaire's findings will be kept private and confidential for academic purposes and individual respondents to this questionnaire will not be identified. I am honoured if you will spend your time to complete this questionnaire in due time.

Please tick (✓) in the spaces provided to indicate your responses.

Appendix A: Questionnaire for the Research Project

Section A: Online Purchase Behaviour

First, I would like to gauge your Online Purchase Behaviour.

Q1) How frequently do you purchase things online?
☐ At least once a week
☐ Once in every 1 – 4 weeks
☐ Once in every 1 – 3 months
☐ Once in every 4 – 12 months
☐ Once every more than 12 months or none.

Q2) What are the barriers affecting your actions when purchasing things online?
☐ Financial barriers
☐ Technical barriers
☐ Organizational barriers
☐ Behavioural barriers
☐ Legal and regulatory barriers

Q3) How much experience do you have with online shopping?
☐ Very High
☐ High
☐ Some
☐ Little
☐ Very Little

Q4) How significant is the impact of your online purchase intentions on your online purchase behaviour?

☐ Very significant
☐ Quite Significant
☐ Moderately Significant
☐ Quite Insignificant
☐ Very Insignificant

Appendix A: Questionnaire for the Research Project

Section B: Push Factors

Next, I would like to know the factors that drive you to purchase things online.

Kindly indicate your agreeableness to each of the statements below from the scale of 1 – 7.

Scale

1 = Very Strongly Agree   2 = Strongly Agree   3 = Slightly Agree
4 = Neutral
5 = Slightly Disagree   6 = Strongly Disagree   7 = Very Strongly Disagree

		1	2	3	4	5	6	7
1	A higher purchasing power has a positive impact on my online purchase intention when I can bargain and get better prices for products online.							
2	A higher purchasing power increases the goods I consume with online shopping.							

		1	2	3	4	5	6	7
3	A higher purchasing power increases the likelihood of me conducting e-commerce activities, which in turn, increases my intention to purchase things online.							
4	My online purchase intention is motivated by the fact online shopping allows me to save time by allowing me to shop at home.							
5	Online purchases are more time saving than other forms of purchases to me and this affects my online purchase intention.							
6	Online purchases are more time saving to me as they can be done just by getting an idea of what products are to be purchased and clicking on a mouse.							

Appendix A: Questionnaire for the Research Project

		1	2	3	4	5	6	7
7	Perceived risk leads me to a fear of uncertainty which can cause serious outcomes and negative intentions when I make online purchases.							
8	Perceived risk can cause me to hesitate when making online purchases.							
9	Perceived risk leads me to fear that I may purchase the wrong products with online shopping, negatively affecting my online purchase intention.							
10	Perceived risk is more likely to occur to and affect me when I conduct online purchases as opposed to traditional purchases.							

		1	2	3	4	5	6	7
11	Increased frequency of purchasing things online causes me to have a higher intention to shop online because of technology familiarity with increased frequency of purchasing things online.							
12	Increased frequency of purchasing things online encourages me to shop online based on usefulness.							
13	Increased frequency of purchasing things online encourages me to shop online based on level of experience.							

Appendix A: Questionnaire for the Research Project

Section C: Pull Factors

In this section, I would like to know the factors that attract you to purchase things online.

Kindly indicate your agreeableness to each of the statements below from the scale of 1 – 7.

		1	2	3	4	5	6	7
1	When shopping online for products, I trust the online shopping vendor and the vendor's website before shopping.							
2	Trust helps me to reduce uncertainty when I make online purchases of products.							
3	Business trustworthiness is needed in order to get me to purchase products.							
4	Competence, integrity and benevolence improves my trust and intention in online purchases.							

		1	2	3	4	5	6	7
5	I try to make comparisons between products if they are sold online to save money compared to other purchase methods before purchasing products.							
6	I am positively influenced in online purchase intention by price comparison websites when shopping online.							
7	Price comparison encourages me to repurchase products with online social media.							
8	Advertising can improve my perceived value towards online shops, which leads to online purchase intention.							
9	Advertisements of a product, after being viewed by me, shape my actions in buying the advertised product online.							

Appendix A: Questionnaire for the Research Project

		1	2	3	4	5	6	7
10	Based on precise targeting to me, advertising increases my intention to purchase products online.							
11	I buy products online with the assistance of brand names instead of product information.							
12	Brand names provide visual and mental familiarity for products that I will buy online before I decide to buy these products.							
13	Brand names encourage me to buy products online based on association of brand name with high quality products.							
14	I tend to process the brand names of products for recognition before purchasing them online.							

Section D: Online Purchase Intention

Next, I would like to know your online purchase intention.

Kindly indicate your agreeableness to each of the statements below from the scale of 1 – 7.

		1	2	3	4	5	6	7
1	I have a positive attitude towards purchasing things online.							
2	I intend to purchase things online based on predictable usefulness.							
3	I intend to purchase things based on utilitarianism, enjoyment and ease of use.							
4	I intend to purchase things based on situational factors.							

Appendix A: Questionnaire for the Research Project

Section E: Demographics

―――

1. Gender
☐ Male
☐ Female

2. Ethnicity
☐ Malay
☐ Indian
☐ Chinese
☐ Others

3. Age Group
☐ < 13 years old
☐ 13 to 20 years old
☐ 21 to 40 years old
☐ 41 to 50 years old
☐ 51 to 70 years old
☐ Older than 70 years old

4. Highest Education Level

☐ SPM and below

☐ STPM / Foundation Studies / College Diploma / Professional Course/ Vocational Studies

☐ Bachelor's Degree

☐ Master's Degree / PHD

☐ Higher than Master's Degree / PHD

5. Employment Status

☐ Public sector employee

☐ Private sector employee

☐ Student

☐ Unemployed / Homemaker / Housewife

☐ Self-employed / Business / Other organization owner

6. Income Status

☐ < RM100,000

☐ RM100,000 to RM500,000

☐ RM500,000 to RM1,000,000

☐ > RM1,000,000

You have reach the end of this study.

Thank you very much for your time.
Your participation is much appreciated.

APPENDIX B

SPSS Results for skewness and kurtosis

Descriptives for Push Factors (including skewness and kurtosis)

			Statistic	Std. Error
H1	Mean		3.10	.074
	95% Confidence Interval for Mean	Lower Bound	2.95	
		Upper Bound	3.24	
	5% Trimmed Mean		3.02	
	Median		3.00	
	Variance		2.321	
	Std. Deviation		1.524	
	Minimum		1	
	Maximum		7	
	Range		6	
	Interquartile Range		2	
	Skewness		.481	.119
	Kurtosis		-.208	.237

Appendix B: SPSS Results for skewness and kurtosis

			Statistic	Std. Error
H2	Mean		3.31	.073
	95% Confidence Interval for Mean	Lower Bound	3.16	
		Upper Bound	3.45	
	5% Trimmed Mean		3.25	
	Median		3.00	
	Variance		2.275	
	Std. Deviation		1.508	
	Minimum		1	
	Maximum		7	
	Range		6	
	Interquartile Range		2	
	Skewness		.424	.119
	Kurtosis		-.278	.237

			Statistic	Std. Error
H3	Mean		3.37	.070
	95% Confidence Interval for Mean	Lower Bound	3.23	
		Upper Bound	3.50	
	5% Trimmed Mean		3.32	
	Median		3.00	
	Variance		2.053	
	Std. Deviation		1.433	
	Minimum		1	
	Maximum		7	
	Range		6	
	Interquartile Range		2	
	Skewness		.323	.119
	Kurtosis		-.205	.237

Appendix B: SPSS Results for skewness and kurtosis

			Statistic	Std. Error
H4	Mean		3.21	.084
	95% Confidence Interval for Mean	Lower Bound	3.04	
		Upper Bound	3.37	
	5% Trimmed Mean		3.12	
	Median		3.00	
	Variance		2.992	
	Std. Deviation		1.730	
	Minimum		1	
	Maximum		7	
	Range		6	
	Interquartile Range		2	
	Skewness		.553	.119
	Kurtosis		-.668	.237

		Statistic	Std. Error
	Mean	3.25	.083
	95% Confidence Interval for Mean — Lower Bound	3.08	
	95% Confidence Interval for Mean — Upper Bound	3.41	
	5% Trimmed Mean	3.16	
	Median	3.00	
	Variance	2.939	
H5	Std. Deviation	1.714	
	Minimum	1	
	Maximum	7	
	Range	6	
	Interquartile Range	2	
	Skewness	.525	.119
	Kurtosis	-.613	.237

Appendix B: SPSS Results for skewness and kurtosis

			Statistic	Std. Error
	Mean		3.17	.082
	95% Confidence Interval for Mean	Lower Bound	3.01	
		Upper Bound	3.33	
	5% Trimmed Mean		3.08	
	Median		3.00	
	Variance		2.822	
H6	Std. Deviation		1.680	
	Minimum		1	
	Maximum		7	
	Range		6	
	Interquartile Range		2	
	Skewness		.530	.119
	Kurtosis		-.538	.237

			Statistic	Std. Error
H7	Mean		3.36	.076
	95% Confidence Interval for Mean	Lower Bound	3.21	
		Upper Bound	3.51	
	5% Trimmed Mean		3.30	
	Median		3.00	
	Variance		2.457	
	Std. Deviation		1.567	
	Minimum		1	
	Maximum		7	
	Range		6	
	Interquartile Range		2	
	Skewness		.370	.119
	Kurtosis		-.502	.237

Appendix B: SPSS Results for skewness and kurtosis

			Statistic	Std. Error
	Mean		3.18	.079
	95% Confidence Interval for Mean	Lower Bound	3.03	
		Upper Bound	3.34	
	5% Trimmed Mean		3.11	
	Median		3.00	
	Variance		2.619	
H8	Std. Deviation		1.618	
	Minimum		1	
	Maximum		7	
	Range		6	
	Interquartile Range		2	
	Skewness		.466	.119
	Kurtosis		-.496	.237

			Statistic	Std. Error
H9	Mean		3.08	.077
	95% Confidence Interval for Mean	Lower Bound	2.93	
		Upper Bound	3.23	
	5% Trimmed Mean		3.00	
	Median		3.00	
	Variance		2.520	
	Std. Deviation		1.588	
	Minimum		1	
	Maximum		7	
	Range		6	
	Interquartile Range		2	
	Skewness		.512	.119
	Kurtosis		-.459	.237

Appendix B: SPSS Results for skewness and kurtosis

			Statistic	Std. Error
H10	Mean		3.22	.071
	95% Confidence Interval for Mean	Lower Bound	3.08	
		Upper Bound	3.36	
	5% Trimmed Mean		3.16	
	Median		3.00	
	Variance		2.143	
	Std. Deviation		1.464	
	Minimum		1	
	Maximum		7	
	Range		6	
	Interquartile Range		2	
	Skewness		.428	.119
	Kurtosis		-.272	.237

			Statistic	Std. Error
H11	Mean		3.24	.069
	95% Confidence Interval for Mean	Lower Bound	3.11	
		Upper Bound	3.38	
	5% Trimmed Mean		3.18	
	Median		3.00	
	Variance		2.003	
	Std. Deviation		1.415	
	Minimum		1	
	Maximum		7	
	Range		6	
	Interquartile Range		2	
	Skewness		.433	.119
	Kurtosis		-.092	.237

Appendix B: SPSS Results for skewness and kurtosis

			Statistic	Std. Error
H12	Mean		3.36	.074
	95% Confidence Interval for Mean	Lower Bound	3.22	
		Upper Bound	3.51	
	5% Trimmed Mean		3.32	
	Median		3.00	
	Variance		2.350	
	Std. Deviation		1.533	
	Minimum		1	
	Maximum		7	
	Range		6	
	Interquartile Range		2	
	Skewness		.383	.119
	Kurtosis		-.552	.237

			Statistic	Std. Error
H13	Mean		3.30	.074
	95% Confidence Interval for Mean	Lower Bound	3.16	
		Upper Bound	3.45	
	5% Trimmed Mean		3.25	
	Median		3.00	
	Variance		2.292	
	Std. Deviation		1.514	
	Minimum		1	
	Maximum		7	
	Range		6	
	Interquartile Range		2	
	Skewness		.419	.119
	Kurtosis		-.485	.237

Appendix B: SPSS Results for skewness and kurtosis

Descriptives for Pull Factors (including skewness and kurtosis)

			Statistic	Std. Error
I1	Mean		3.24	.076
	95% Confidence Interval for Mean	Lower Bound	3.09	
		Upper Bound	3.39	
	5% Trimmed Mean		3.18	
	Median		3.00	
	Variance		2.424	
	Std. Deviation		1.557	
	Minimum		1	
	Maximum		7	
	Range		6	
	Interquartile Range		2	
	Skewness		.410	.119
	Kurtosis		-.429	.237

Appendix B: SPSS Results for skewness and kurtosis

		Statistic	Std. Error
Mean		2.98	.077
95% Confidence Interval for Mean	Lower Bound	2.83	
	Upper Bound	3.13	
5% Trimmed Mean		2.88	
Median		3.00	
Variance		2.543	
Std. Deviation		1.595	
Minimum		1	
Maximum		7	
Range		6	
Interquartile Range		2	
Skewness		.621	.119
Kurtosis		-.210	.237

		Statistic	Std. Error
13	Mean	2.95	.085
	95% Confidence Interval for Mean — Lower Bound	2.78	
	95% Confidence Interval for Mean — Upper Bound	3.11	
	5% Trimmed Mean	2.83	
	Median	2.50	
	Variance	3.044	
	Std. Deviation	1.745	
	Minimum	1	
	Maximum	7	
	Range	6	
	Interquartile Range	3	
	Skewness	.679	.119
	Kurtosis	-.522	.237

Appendix B: SPSS Results for skewness and kurtosis

		Statistic	Std. Error
Mean		3.04	.079
95% Confidence Interval for Mean	Lower Bound	2.89	
	Upper Bound	3.20	
5% Trimmed Mean		2.95	
Median		3.00	
Variance		2.676	
Std. Deviation		1.636	
Minimum		1	
Maximum		7	
Range		6	
Interquartile Range		2	
Skewness		.595	.119
Kurtosis		-.411	.237

		Statistic	Std. Error
	Mean	2.92	.092
95% Confidence Interval for Mean	Lower Bound	2.74	
	Upper Bound	3.10	
	5% Trimmed Mean	2.79	
	Median	2.00	
	Variance	3.553	
I5	Std. Deviation	1.885	
	Minimum	1	
	Maximum	7	
	Range	6	
	Interquartile Range	3	
	Skewness	.766	.119
	Kurtosis	-.548	.237

Appendix B: SPSS Results for skewness and kurtosis

		Statistic	Std. Error
Mean		3.10	.088
95% Confidence Interval for Mean	Lower Bound	2.93	
	Upper Bound	3.27	
5% Trimmed Mean		3.00	
Median		3.00	
Variance		3.292	
Std. Deviation		1.814	
Minimum		1	
Maximum		7	
Range		6	
Interquartile Range		2	
Skewness		.631	.119
Kurtosis		-.601	.237

			Statistic	Std. Error
17	Mean		3.24	.080
	95% Confidence Interval for Mean	Lower Bound	3.08	
		Upper Bound	3.39	
	5% Trimmed Mean		3.15	
	Median		3.00	
	Variance		2.720	
	Std. Deviation		1.649	
	Minimum		1	
	Maximum		7	
	Range		6	
	Interquartile Range		2	
	Skewness		.566	.119
	Kurtosis		-.424	.237

Appendix B: SPSS Results for skewness and kurtosis

		Statistic	Std. Error
	Mean	3.30	.071
95% Confidence Interval for Mean	Lower Bound	3.16	
	Upper Bound	3.44	
	5% Trimmed Mean	3.25	
	Median	3.00	
	Variance	2.134	
I8	Std. Deviation	1.461	
	Minimum	1	
	Maximum	7	
	Range	6	
	Interquartile Range	2	
	Skewness	.316	.119
	Kurtosis	-.322	.237

		Statistic	Std. Error
19	Mean	3.41	.073
	95% Confidence Interval for Mean — Lower Bound	3.26	
	95% Confidence Interval for Mean — Upper Bound	3.55	
	5% Trimmed Mean	3.36	
	Median	3.00	
	Variance	2.242	
	Std. Deviation	1.497	
	Minimum	1	
	Maximum	7	
	Range	6	
	Interquartile Range	2	
	Skewness	.262	.119
	Kurtosis	-.411	.237

Appendix B: SPSS Results for skewness and kurtosis

		Statistic	Std. Error
Mean		3.42	.070
95% Confidence Interval for Mean	Lower Bound	3.28	
	Upper Bound	3.56	
5% Trimmed Mean		3.38	
Median		3.00	
Variance		2.088	
Std. Deviation		1.445	
Minimum		1	
Maximum		7	
Range		6	
Interquartile Range		2	
Skewness		.331	.119
Kurtosis		-.324	.237

I10

			Statistic	Std. Error
I11	Mean		3.60	.080
	95% Confidence Interval for Mean	Lower Bound	3.44	
		Upper Bound	3.76	
	5% Trimmed Mean		3.55	
	Median		4.00	
	Variance		2.742	
	Std. Deviation		1.656	
	Minimum		1	
	Maximum		7	
	Range		6	
	Interquartile Range		3	
	Skewness		.184	.119
	Kurtosis		-.743	.237

Appendix B: SPSS Results for skewness and kurtosis

		Statistic	Std. Error
Mean		3.24	.077
95% Confidence Interval for Mean	Lower Bound	3.09	
	Upper Bound	3.39	
5% Trimmed Mean		3.17	
Median		3.00	
Variance		2.541	
Std. Deviation		1.594	
Minimum		1	
Maximum		7	
Range		6	
Interquartile Range		2	
Skewness		.411	.119
Kurtosis		-.471	.237

		Statistic	Std. Error
Mean		3.31	.078
95% Confidence Interval for Mean	Lower Bound	3.15	
	Upper Bound	3.46	
5% Trimmed Mean		3.24	
Median		3.00	
Variance		2.577	
Std. Deviation		1.605	
Minimum		1	
Maximum		7	
Range		6	
Interquartile Range		2	
Skewness		.439	.119
Kurtosis		-.477	.237

Appendix B: SPSS Results for skewness and kurtosis

		Statistic	Std. Error
Mean		3.33	.080
95% Confidence Interval for Mean	Lower Bound	3.17	
	Upper Bound	3.48	
5% Trimmed Mean		3.25	
Median		3.00	
Variance		2.693	
Std. Deviation		1.641	
Minimum		1	
Maximum		7	
Range		6	
Interquartile Range		2	
Skewness		.433	.119
Kurtosis		-.491	.237

Descriptives for Online Purchase Intention (including skewness and kurtosis)

			Statistic	Std. Error
L1	Mean		3.25	.071
	95% Confidence Interval for Mean	Lower Bound	3.11	
		Upper Bound	3.39	
	5% Trimmed Mean		3.20	
	Median		3.00	
	Variance		2.148	
	Std. Deviation		1.466	
	Minimum		1	
	Maximum		7	
	Range		6	
	Interquartile Range		2	
	Skewness		.413	.119
	Kurtosis		-.327	.237

Appendix B: SPSS Results for skewness and kurtosis

			Statistic	Std. Error
L2	Mean		3.27	.076
	95% Confidence Interval for Mean	Lower Bound	3.12	
		Upper Bound	3.42	
	5% Trimmed Mean		3.21	
	Median		3.00	
	Variance		2.444	
	Std. Deviation		1.563	
	Minimum		1	
	Maximum		7	
	Range		6	
	Interquartile Range		2	
	Skewness		.487	.119
	Kurtosis		-.474	.237

		Statistic	Std. Error
L3	Mean	3.26	.078
	95% Confidence Interval for Mean — Lower Bound	3.10	
	95% Confidence Interval for Mean — Upper Bound	3.41	
	5% Trimmed Mean	3.19	
	Median	3.00	
	Variance	2.565	
	Std. Deviation	1.602	
	Minimum	1	
	Maximum	7	
	Range	6	
	Interquartile Range	2	
	Skewness	.501	.119
	Kurtosis	-.505	.237

Appendix B: SPSS Results for skewness and kurtosis

			Statistic	Std. Error
L4	Mean		3.27	.077
	95% Confidence Interval for Mean	Lower Bound	3.12	
		Upper Bound	3.42	
	5% Trimmed Mean		3.20	
	Median		3.00	
	Variance		2.496	
	Std. Deviation		1.580	
	Minimum		1	
	Maximum		7	
	Range		6	
	Interquartile Range		2	
	Skewness		.454	.119
	Kurtosis		-.442	.237

Why Malaysian Consumers Prefer Online Purchases

APPENDIX C

*Cronbach's Alpha Tests
for all respondents to the project*

Reliability

Scale: ALL VARIABLES

Case Processing Summary

		N	%
Cases	Valid	424	99.8
	Excluded[a]	1	.2
	Total	425	100.0

a. Listwise deletion based on all variables in the procedure.

Reliability Statistics

Cronbach's Alpha	Cronbach's Alpha based on Standardized Items	N of Items
.919	.919	13

Appendix C: Cronbach's Alpha Tests for all respondents to the project

	Item Statistics		
	Mean	Std. Deviation	N
H1	3.10	1.524	424
H2	3.31	1.508	424
H3	3.37	1.433	424
H4	3.21	1.730	424
H5	3.25	1.714	424
H6	3.17	1.680	424
H7	3.36	1.567	424
H8	3.18	1.618	424
H9	3.08	1.588	424
H10	3.22	1.464	424
H11	3.24	1.415	424
H12	3.36	1.533	424
H13	3.30	1.514	424

Item-Total Statistics

	Scale Mean if Item Deleted	Scale Variance if Item Deleted	Corrected Item-Total Correlation	Squared Multiple Correlation	Cronbach's Alpha if Item Deleted
H1	39.05	180.291	.663	.543	.913
H2	38.84	181.686	.634	.565	.914
H3	38.78	185.393	.571	.484	.916
H4	38.94	175.670	.678	.569	.912
H5	38.90	175.671	.685	.670	.912
H6	38.98	176.340	.685	.626	.912
H7	38.79	180.932	.625	.637	.914
H8	38.96	179.450	.638	.669	.914
H9	39.06	180.741	.620	.573	.914
H10	38.93	182.588	.632	.526	.914
H11	38.91	181.878	.677	.572	.912
H12	38.78	179.054	.690	.580	.912
H13	38.84	179.153	.698	.577	.911

Appendix C: Cronbach's Alpha Tests for all respondents to the project

Scale Statistics			
Mean	Variance	Std. Deviation	N of Items
42.15	209.733	14.482	13

RELIABILITY
 /VARIABLES = I1 I2 I3 I4 I5 I6 I7 I8 I9 I10 I11 I12 I13 I14
 /SCALE ('ALL VARIABLES') ALL
 /MODEL = ALPHA
 /STATISTICS = DESCRIPTIVE SCALE CORR
 /SUMMARY = TOTAL.

Reliability

Scale: ALL VARIABLES

Case Processing Summary

		N	%
Cases	Valid	424	99.8
	Excluded[a]	1	.2
	Total	425	100.0

a. Listwise deletion based on all variables in the procedure.

Reliability Statistics

Cronbach's Alpha	Cronbach's Alpha based on Standardized Items	N of Items
.936	.937	14

Appendix C: Cronbach's Alpha Tests for all respondents to the project

Item Statistics

	Mean	Std. Deviation	N
I1	3.24	1.557	424
I2	2.98	1.595	424
I3	2.95	1.745	424
I4	3.04	1.636	424
I5	2.92	1.885	424
I6	3.10	1.814	424
I7	3.24	1.649	424
I8	3.30	1.461	424
I9	3.41	1.497	424
I10	3.42	1.445	424
I11	3.60	1.656	424
I12	3.24	1.594	424
I13	3.31	1.605	424
I14	3.33	1.641	424

Item-Total Statistics

	Scale Mean if Item Deleted	Scale Variance if Item Deleted	Corrected Item-Total Correlation	Squared Multiple Correlation	Cronbach's Alpha if Item Deleted
I1	41.82	256.206	.543	.377	.936
I2	42.08	244.597	.773	.747	.930
I3	42.11	239.666	.795	.802	.929
I4	42.01	243.291	.778	.747	.929
I5	42.14	239.920	.723	.729	.931
I6	41.96	241.138	.732	.628	.931
I7	41.82	249.120	.650	.529	.933
I8	41.76	251.619	.689	.643	.932
I9	41.65	252.180	.657	.647	.933
I10	41.64	254.932	.621	.565	.934
I11	41.46	254.717	.534	.467	.936
I12	41.82	246.228	.738	.715	.931
I13	41.75	246.196	.733	.688	.931
I14	41.73	245.647	.726	.685	.931

Appendix C: Cronbach's Alpha Tests for all respondents to the project

Scale Statistics			
Mean	Variance	Std. Deviation	N of Items
45.06	285.682	16.902	14

```
RELIABILITY
 /VARIABLES = L1 L2 L3 L4
 /SCALE ('ALL VARIABLES') ALL
 /MODEL = ALPHA
 /STATISTICS = DESCRIPTIVE SCALE CORR
 /SUMMARY = TOTAL.
```

Reliability

Scale: ALL VARIABLES

Case Processing Summary

		N	%
Cases	Valid	424	99.8
	Excluded[a]	1	.2
	Total	425	100.0

a. Listwise deletion based on all variables in the procedure.

Reliability Statistics

Cronbach's Alpha	Cronbach's Alpha based on Standardized Items	N of Items
.889	.889	4

Appendix C: Cronbach's Alpha Tests for all respondents to the project

Item Statistics

	Mean	Std. Deviation	N
L1	3.25	1.466	424
L2	3.27	1.563	424
L3	3.26	1.602	424
L4	3.27	1.580	424

Item-Total Statistics

	Scale Mean if Item Deleted	Scale Variance if Item Deleted	Corrected Item-Total Correlation	Squared Multiple Correlation	Cronbach's Alpha if Item Deleted
L1	9.80	17.830	.725	.555	.869
L2	9.78	16.289	.810	.664	.836
L3	9.80	16.398	.770	.600	.852
L4	9.78	17.045	.722	.531	.870

Scale Statistics

Mean	Variance	Std. Deviation	N of Items
13.05	28.954	5.381	4

APPENDIX D

Multiple Regression Analysis

REGRESSION
  /MISSING LISTWISE
  /STATISTICS COEFF OUTS R ANOVA
  /CRITERIA = PIN (.05) POUT (.10)
  /NOORIGIN
  /DEPENDENT L5
  /METHOD = ENTER H14
  /RESIDUALS HISTOGRAM (ZRESID) NORMPROB (ZRESID).

Variables Entered/Removed[a]

Model	Variables Entered	Variables Removed	Method
1	H14[b]	.	Enter

a. Dependent Variable: L5
b. All requested variables entered.

Model Summary[b]

Model	R	R Square	Adjusted R Square	Std. Error of the Estimate
1	.655[a]	.429	.428	1.016

a. Predictors: (Constant), H14
b. Dependent Variable: L5

ANOVA[a]

Model		Sum of Squares	df	Mean Square	F	Sig.
1	Regression	326.092	1	326.092	316.138	.000[b]
	Residual	434.256	421	1.031		
	Total	760.349	422			

a. Dependent Variable: L5
b. Predictors: (Constant), H14

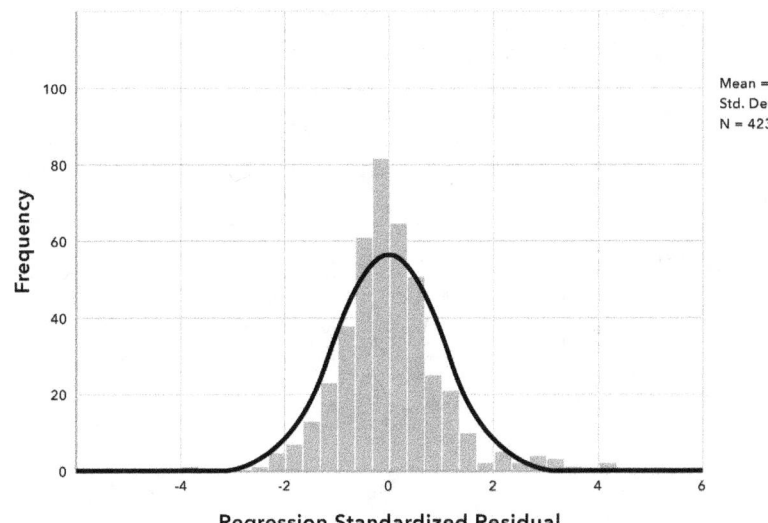

Histogram
Dependent Variable: L5

Mean = 9.65E - 16
Std. Dev. = 0.999
N = 423

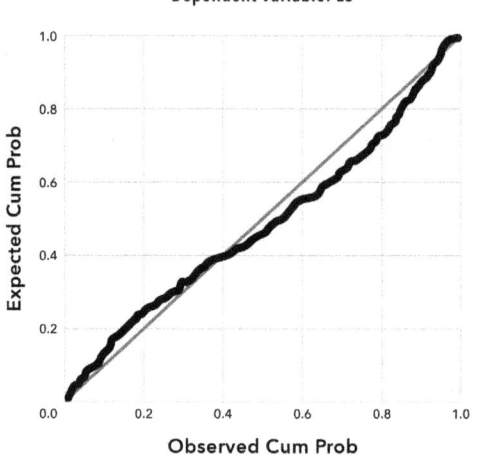

Normal P-P Plot of Regression Standardized Residual
Dependent Variable: L5

Coefficients[a]

Model		Unstandardized Coefficients		Standardized Coefficients	t	Sig.	95.0% Confidence Interval for B		Collinearity Statistics	
		B	Std. Error	Beta			Lower Bound	Upper Bound	Tolerance	VIF
1	(Constant)	.697	.153		4.561	.000	.397	.998		
	H14	.792	.045	.655	17.780	.000	.704	.880	1.000	1.000

a. Dependent Variable: L5

Appendix D: Multiple Regression Analysis

Collinearity Diagnostics[a]

Model	Dimension	Eigenvalue	Condition Index	Variance Proportions	
				(Constant)	H14
1	1	1.946	1.000	.03	.03
	2	.054	6.024	.97	.97

a. Dependent Variable: L5

Residuals Statistics[a]

	Minimum	Maximum	Mean	Std. Deviation	N
Predicted Value	1.49	6.12	3.27	.879	423
Std. Predicted Value	-2.025	3.242	.000	1.000	423
Standard Error of Predicted Value	.049	.168	.067	.020	423
Adjusted Predicted Value	1.47	6.09	3.27	.879	423
Residual	-3.779	4.286	.000	1.014	423
Std. Residual	-3.721	4.220	.000	.999	423
Stud. Residual	-3.738	4.229	.000	1.001	423
Deleted Residual	-3.814	4.305	.000	1.019	423
Stud. Deleted Residual	-3.797	4.317	.001	1.007	423
Mahal. Distance	.000	10.512	.998	1.414	423
Cook's Distance	.000	.066	.002	.006	423
Centered Leverage Value	.000	.025	.002	.003	423

a. Dependent Variable: L5

REGRESSION
 /MISSING LISTWISE
 /STATISTICS COEFF OUTS R ANOVA
 /CRITERIA = PIN (.05) POUT (.10)
 /NOORIGIN
 /DEPENDENT L5
 /METHOD = ENTER I15
 /RESIDUALS HISTOGRAM(ZRESID) NORMPROB(ZRESID).

Variables Entered/Removed[a]

Model	Variables Entered	Variables Removed	Method
1	I15[b]	.	Enter

a. Dependent Variable: L5
b. All requested variables entered.

Model Summary[b]

Model	R	R Square	Adjusted R Square	Std. Error of the Estimate
1	.785[a]	.616	.616	.834

a. Predictors: (Constant), I15
b. Dependent Variable: L5

Appendix D: Multiple Regression Analysis

ANOVA[a]

Model		Sum of Squares	df	Mean Square	F	Sig.
1	Regression	471.881	1	471.881	678.242	.000[b]
	Residual	293.603	422	.696		
	Total	765.485	423			

a. Dependent Variable: L5
b. Predictors: (Constant), I15

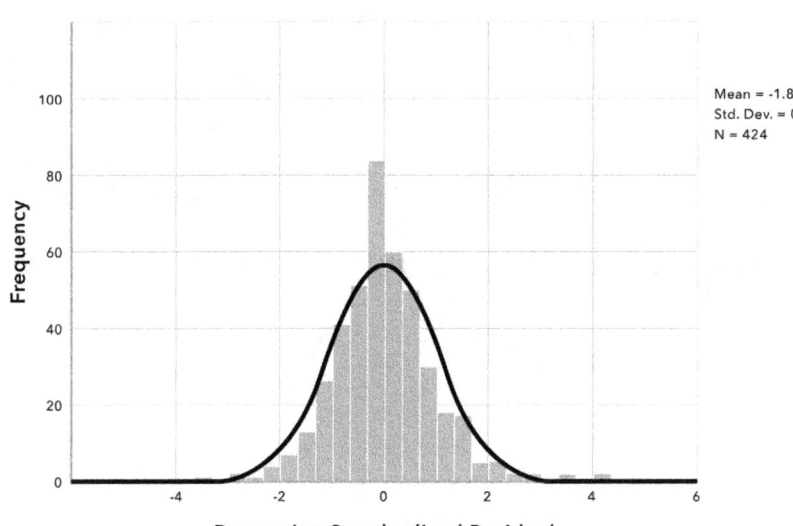

Histogram
Dependent Variable: L5

Mean = -1.84E - 15
Std. Dev. = 0.999
N = 424

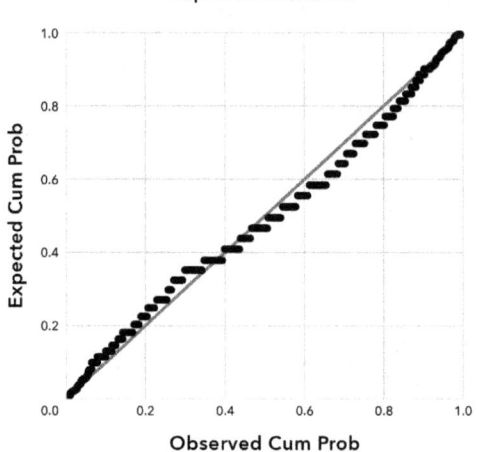

Normal P-P Plot of Regression Standardized Residual
Dependent Variable: L5

Coefficients[a]

Model		Unstandardized Coefficients		Standardized Coefficients	t	Sig.	95.0% Confidence Interval for B		Collinearity Statistics	
		B	Std. Error	Beta			Lower Bound	Upper Bound	Tolerance	VIF
1	(Constant)	.448	.115		3.879	.000	.221	.675		
	I15	.875	.034	.785	26.043	.000	.809	.941	1.000	1.000

a. Dependent Variable: L5

Appendix D: Multiple Regression Analysis

Collinearity Diagnostics[a]

Model	Dimension	Eigenvalue	Condition Index	Variance Proportions	
				(Constant)	I15
1	1	1.936	1.000	.03	.03
	2	.064	5.519	.97	.97

a. Dependent Variable: L5

Residuals Statistics[a]

	Minimum	Maximum	Mean	Std. Deviation	N
Predicted Value	1.32	6.57	3.26	1.056	424
Std. Predicted Value	-1.838	3.132	.000	1.000	424
Standard Error of Predicted Value	.041	.133	.055	.016	424
Adjusted Predicted Value	1.32	6.56	3.26	1.056	424
Residual	-3.010	3.490	.000	.833	424
Std. Residual	-3.608	4.184	.000	.999	424
Stud. Residual	-3.616	4.199	.000	1.001	424
Deleted Residual	-3.023	3.515	.000	.837	424
Stud. Deleted Residual	-3.669	4.284	.001	1.006	424
Mahal. Distance	.000	9.811	.998	1.301	424
Cook's Distance	.000	.066	.002	.006	424
Centered Leverage Value	.000	.023	.002	.003	424

a. Dependent Variable: L5

REGRESSION
/MISSING LISTWISE
/STATISTICS COEFF OUTS CI(95) R ANOVA COLLIN TOL CHANGE
/CRITERIA = PIN (.05) POUT (.10)
/NOORIGIN
/DEPENDENT L5
/METHOD = ENTER H14
/METHOD = ENTER Age
/SAVE PRED COOK LEVER SRESID SDRESID.

Variables Entered/Removed[a]

Model	Variables Entered	Variables Removed	Method
1	H14[b]	.	Enter
2	Age[b]	.	Enter

a. Dependent Variable: L5
b. All requested variables entered.

Model Summary[c]

Model	R	R Square	Adjusted R Square	Std. Error of the Estimate	R Square Change	F Change	df1	df2	Sig. F Change
1	.655[a]	.429	.428	1.016	.429	316.138	1	421	.000
2	.656[b]	.430	.427	1.016	.001	.840	1	420	.360

a. Predictors: (Constant), H14
b. Predictors: (Constant), H14, Age
c. Dependent Variable: L5

Appendix D: Multiple Regression Analysis

ANOVA[a]

Model		Sum of Squares	df	Mean Square	F	Sig.
1	Regression	326.092	1	326.092	316.138	.000[b]
	Residual	434.256	421	1.031		
	Total	760.349	422			
2	Regression	326.959	2	163.480	158.429	.000[c]
	Residual	433.390	420	1.032		
	Total	760.349	422			

a. Dependent Variable: L5
b. Predictors: (Constant), H14
c. Predictors: (Constant), H14, Age

Coefficients[a]

Model		Unstandardized Coefficients		Standardized Coefficients	t	Sig.	95.0% Confidence Interval for B		Collinearity Statistics	
		B	Std. Error	Beta			Lower Bound	Upper Bound	Tolerance	VIF
1	(Constant)	.697	.153		4.561	.000	.397	.998		
	H14	.792	.045	.655	17.780	.000	.704	.880	1.000	1.000
2	(Constant)	.894	.263		3.395	.001	.376	1.411		
	H14	.794	.045	.656	17.800	.000	.706	.881	.998	1.002
	Age	-.077	.084	-.034	-.916	.360	-.242	.088	.998	1.002

a. Dependent Variable: L5

Excluded Variables[a]

Model		Beta In	t	Sig.	Partial Correlation	Change Statistics		
						Tolerance	VIF	Minimum Tolerance
1	Age	-.034b	-.916	.360	-.045	.998	1.002	.998

a. Dependent Variable: L5
b. Predictors in the Model: (Constant), H14

Appendix D: Multiple Regression Analysis

Collinearity Diagnostics[a]

Model	Dimension	Eigenvalue	Condition Index	Variance Proportions		
				(Constant)	H14	Age
1	1	1.946	1.000	.03	.03	
	2	.054	6.024	.97	.97	
2	1	2.899	1.000	.00	.01	.01
	2	.079	6.053	.03	.85	.18
	3	.022	11.536	.97	.14	.82

a. Dependent Variable: L5

Residuals Statistics[a]

	Minimum	Maximum	Mean	Std. Deviation	N
Predicted Value	1.46	6.10	3.27	.880	423
Std. Predicted Value	-2.059	3.212	.000	1.000	423
Standard Error of Predicted Value	.058	.215	.082	.025	423
Adjusted Predicted Value	1.44	6.07	3.27	.880	423
Residual	-3.830	4.240	.000	1.013	423
Std. Residual	-3.771	4.174	.000	.998	423
Stud. Residual	-3.794	4.188	.000	1.001	423
Deleted Residual	-3.878	4.269	.000	1.020	423
Stud. Deleted Residual	-3.856	4.273	.001	1.007	423
Mahal. Distance	.401	17.840	1.995	2.454	423
Cook's Distance	.000	.060	.002	.005	423
Centered Leverage Value	.001	.042	.005	.006	423

a. Dependent Variable: L5

Appendix D: Multiple Regression Analysis

REGRESSION

/MISSING LISTWISE
/STATISTICS COEFF OUTS CI (95) R ANOVA COLLIN TOL CHANGE
/CRITERIA = PIN (.05) POUT (.10)
/NOORIGIN
/DEPENDENT L5
/METHOD = ENTER I15
/METHOD = ENTER Age
/SAVE PRED COOK LEVER SRESID SDRESID.

Model Summary[c]

Model	R	R Square	Adjusted R Square	Std. Error of the Estimate	Change Statistics				
					R Square Change	F Change	df1	df2	Sig. F Change
1	.785[a]	.616	.616	.834	.616	678.242	1	422	.000
2	.787[b]	.619	.617	.833	.002	2.476	1	421	.116

a. Predictors: (Constant), I15
b. Predictors: (Constant), I15, Age
c. Dependent Variable: L5

ANOVA[a]

Model		Sum of Squares	df	Mean Square	F	Sig.
1	Regression	471.881	1	471.881	678.242	.000[b]
	Residual	293.603	422	.696		
	Total	765.485	423			
2	Regression	473.598	2	236.799	341.546	.000[c]
	Residual	291.886	421	.693		
	Total	765.485	423			

a. Dependent Variable: L5
b. Predictors: (Constant), I15
c. Predictors: (Constant), I15, Age

Appendix D: Multiple Regression Analysis

Coefficients[a]

Model		Unstandardized Coefficients		Standardized Coefficients	t	Sig.	95.0% Confidence Interval for B		Collinearity Statistics	
		B	Std. Error	Beta			Lower Bound	Upper Bound	Tolerance	VIF
1	(Constant)	.448	.115		3.879	.000	.221	.675		
	I15	.875	.034	.785	26.043	.000	.809	.941	1.000	1.000
2	(Constant)	.724	.210		3.449	.001	.311	1.136		
	I15	.877	.034	.787	26.134	.000	.811	.943	.998	1.002
	Age	-.108	.069	-.047	-1.574	.116	-.243	.027	.998	1.002

a. Dependent Variable: L5

Excluded Variables[a]

Model		Beta In	t	Sig.	Partial Correlation	Change Statistics		
						Tolerance	VIF	Minimum Tolerance
1	Age	-.047[b]	-1.574	.116	-.076	.998	1.002	.998

a. Dependent Variable: L5
b. Predictors in the Model: (Constant), I15

Collinearity Diagnostics[a]

Model	Dimension	Eigenvalue	Condition Index	Variance Proportions		
				(Constant)	I15	Age
1	1	1.936	1.000	.03	.03	
	2	.064	5.519	.97	.97	
2	1	2.887	1.000	.00	.01	.01
	2	.091	5.634	.03	.89	.14
	3	.022	11.356	.96	.10	.86

a. Dependent Variable: L5

Appendix D: Multiple Regression Analysis

Residuals Statistics[a]

	Minimum	Maximum	Mean	Std. Deviation	N
Predicted Value	1.28	6.54	3.26	1.058	424
Std. Predicted Value	-1.878	3.098	.000	1.000	424
Standard Error of Predicted Value	.048	.180	.067	.020	424
Adjusted Predicted Value	1.28	6.53	3.26	1.058	424
Residual	-2.972	3.426	.000	.831	424
Std. Residual	-3.570	4.115	.000	.998	424
Stud. Residual	-3.579	4.135	.000	1.001	424
Deleted Residual	-2.988	3.459	.000	.837	424
Stud. Deleted Residual	-3.631	4.216	.001	1.006	424
Mahal. Distance	.400	18.867	1.995	2.421	424
Cook's Distance	.000	.072	.002	.006	424
Centered Leverage Value	.001	.045	.005	.006	424

a. Dependent Variable: L5

Why Malaysian Consumers Prefer Online Purchases

APPENDIX E

Demographics of the respondents

Figure E1: Gender of the respondents

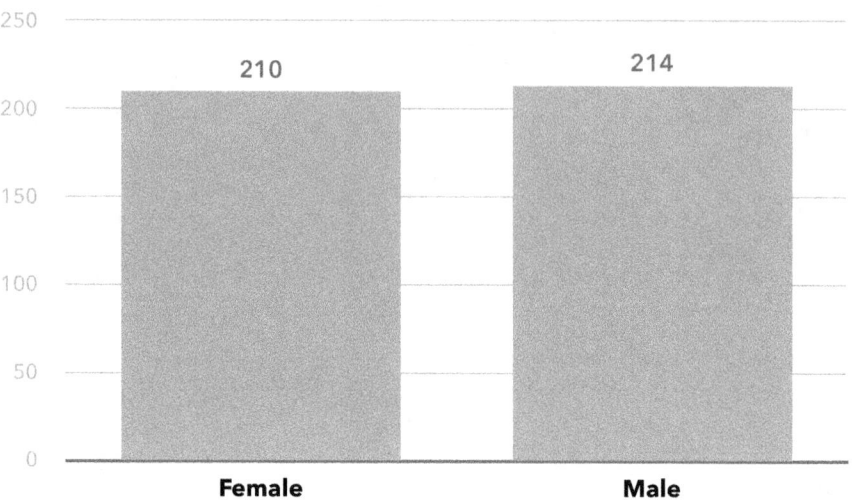

Figure E2: Ethnicity of the respondents

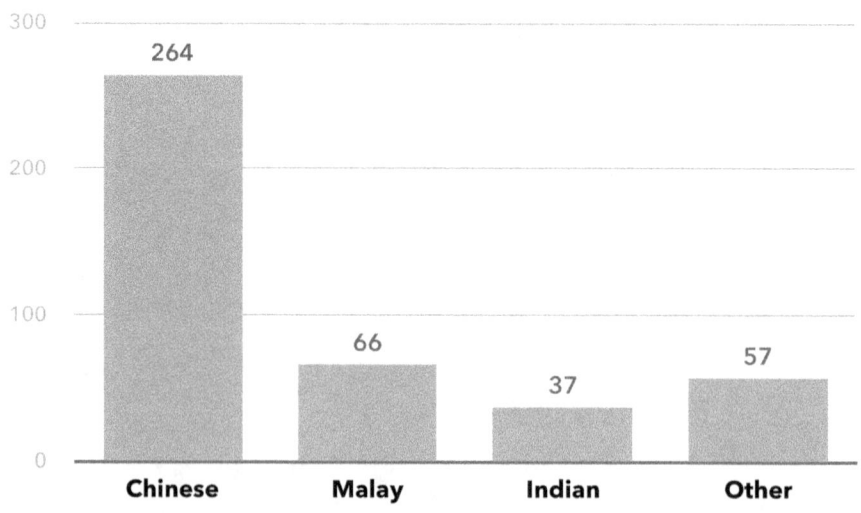

Appendix E: Demographics of the respondents

Figure E3: Employment Status of the respondents

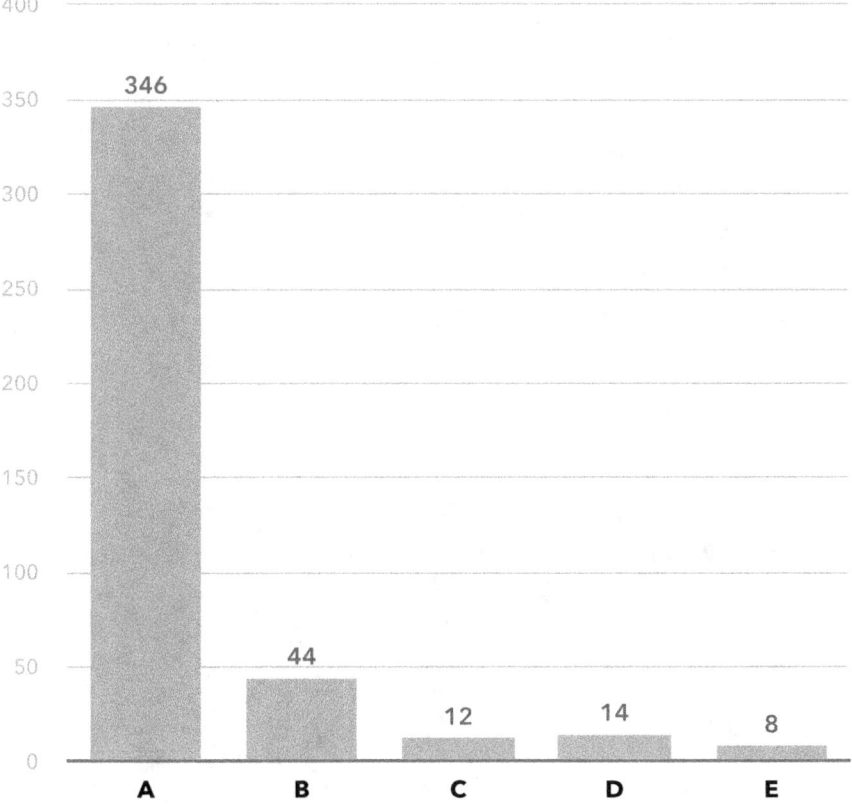

A	Students
B	Private Sector
C	Self-employed / Business / Other Organization Owners
D	Unemployed, Homemakers, Housewives, or Retirees
E	Public Sector

Figure E4: Highest Education Level of the respondents

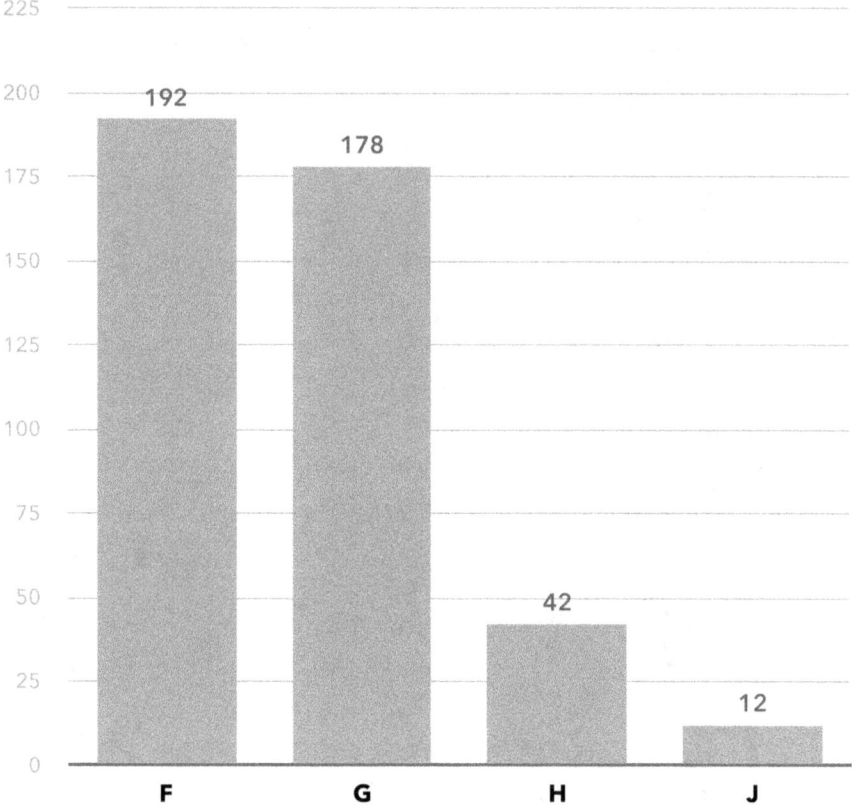

F	Bachelor's Degree
G	STPM / Foundation Studies / College Diploma / Professional Course / Vocational Studies
H	SPM or lower educational qualifications
J	Master's Degree or higher educational qualifications

Appendix E: Demographics of the respondents

Figure E5: Age Group of the respondents

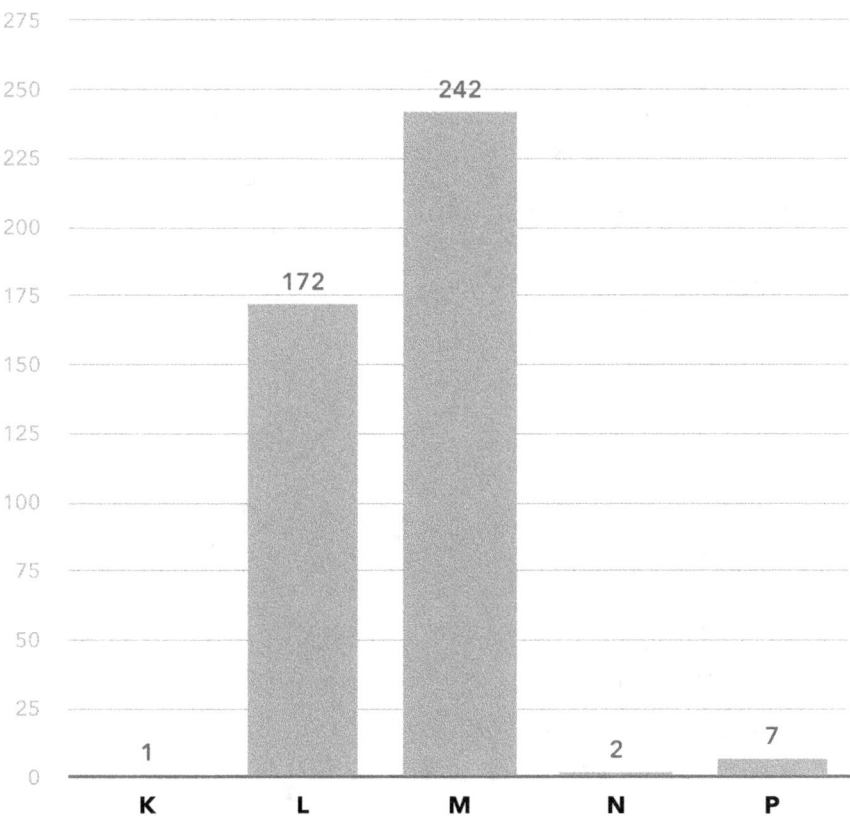

K	Below 13 years of age
L	13 to 20 years of age
M	21 to 40 years of age
N	41 to 50 years of age
P	51 to 70 years of age

Figure E6: Income Per Month of the respondents

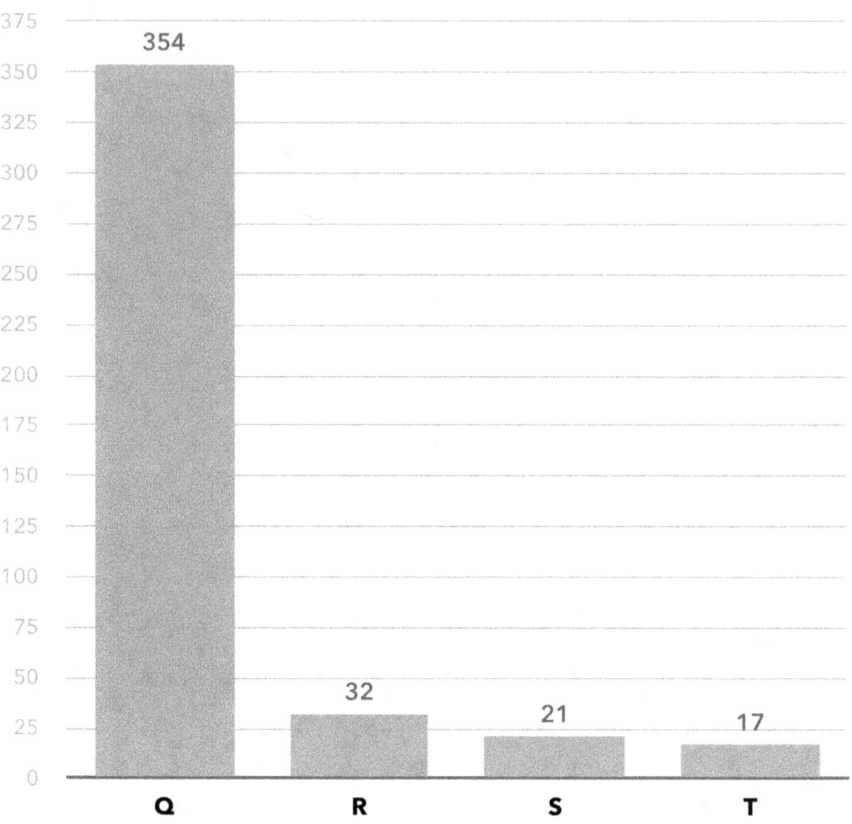

Q	Less than RM3,000
R	RM3,000 to RM5,000
S	Between RM5,000 and RM10,000
T	RM10,000 or higher

Appendix E: Demographics of the respondents

www.ingramcontent.com/pod-product-compliance
Lightning Source LLC
Chambersburg PA
CBHW050052230526
45470CB00004B/1495